Aleksander Jedrosz • Susan Loxley • Ron Holt

KV-512-637

ESSENTIALS

EDEXCEL

GCSE Additional Science

Revision Guide

Contents

How to Use This Guide

This revision guide has been written and developed to help you get the most out of your revision. This guide covers both Foundation and Higher Tier content.

HT Content that will only be tested on the Higher Tier papers appears in a pale yellow tinted box labelled with the **HT** symbol.

- The **coloured page headers** clearly identify the separate units, so that you can revise for each one separately: Unit B2 is red; Unit C2 is purple, and Unit P2 is blue.
- You'll find **key words** in a yellow box on each two-page spread. They are also highlighted in colour within the text. Higher Tier key words are highlighted in orange. Make sure you know and understand all these words before moving on!

- There's a **glossary** at the end of each topic. Each glossary contains the key words from throughout that topic so you can check any definitions you're unsure of.
- There are **practice questions** at the end of each topic so that you can test yourself on what you've just learned. (The answers are given on pages 118–121 so you can mark them yourself.) Please note that the practice questions don't necessarily reflect the type of questions you'll get in the exam. The practice questions are simply to test your knowledge on the information you've just read in the topic.
- The **tick boxes** on the contents page let you track your revision progress: simply put a tick in the box next to each topic when you're confident that you know it.
- Don't just read the guide – **learn actively**! Constantly test yourself without looking at the text.

Good luck with your exams!

How Science Works

How Science Works is an important requirement in the criteria for GCSE Science. It's a set of key concepts, relevant to all areas of science, concerned with the practices and procedures used to collect scientific evidence and the impact it has on society and your life. To reflect Edexcel's approach to How Science Works, and the way this element is taught in schools, these concepts are integrated with the scientific content throughout this guide.

Assessment

As a revision guide, this book focuses on the material that's externally assessed (i.e. tested under exam conditions). It doesn't cover the practical skills assessment and assessment activities, which are marked by your teacher.

There are several assessment routes available, which will include multiple-choice tests and structured question papers.

Inside Living Cells

DNA and Chromosomes

In normal human cells there are **23 pairs** of **chromosomes**. Chromosomes are long, coiled molecules of **DNA**. A **gene** is a section of DNA. Genes **code** for inherited characteristics.

A DNA molecule consists of two coiled **strands** called a **double helix**. The strands are linked by paired **bases**: adenine (A), cytosine (C), guanine (G) and **thymine** (T). Adenine always links to thymine (A–T). Cytosine always links to guanine (C–G). DNA contains the instructions for how the cells link **amino acids** during **protein synthesis**. The instructions are in the form of a code, made up of the four bases.

There are about 20 different amino acids. They're arranged in different combinations to make different **proteins**.

Key Words

Adenine • Amino acid • Aseptic • Base • Coding • Cultivated • Cytosine • DNA • Double helix • Fermentation • Fermenter • Guanine • Insulin • Messenger RNA • Organelle • Polypeptide • Protein • Ribosome • Ribosomal RNA • RNA • Strand • Thymine • Transcription • Translation • Transfer RNA • Triplet

HT Making Proteins

A sequence of three bases in DNA is called a **triplet**. Each triplet codes for one amino acid in a protein. The code is stored in the coding strand of DNA and is copied to produce a molecule of **messenger RNA**. This is **transcription**. **RNA** only has one strand and can move outside the nucleus into the cytoplasm. **Ribosomes** are **organelles** in the cytoplasm of cells, which are involved in protein synthesis. They interpret the code in the RNA to link the amino acids and form a **polypeptide** (a protein). This process is **translation**.

1. DNA unravels at the correct gene.
2. mRNA is made from a copy of the coding strand.
3. mRNA moves from the nucleus to the cytoplasm.
4. The triplet code is interpreted by the ribosomes, which contain **ribosomal RNA** (rRNA) and protein.
5. Amino acids are brought to the ribosome by **transfer RNA** (tRNA).

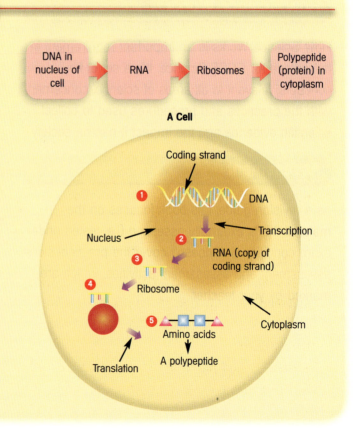

DNA in nucleus of cell → RNA → Ribosomes → Polypeptide (protein) in cytoplasm

A Cell

Coding strand
DNA
Transcription
Nucleus
RNA (copy of coding strand)
Ribosome
Cytoplasm
Amino acids
A polypeptide
Translation

Genetic Engineering

Sections of DNA that code for a specific protein can be transferred into **microorganisms**. The microorganisms then reproduce and make large amounts of the protein.

This method is used to produce many useful substances. For example, bacteria are used to produce large amounts of **insulin**, for use by people with diabetes.

1. The gene for insulin production is identified and removed using a restriction enzyme.
2. Another restriction enzyme is used to cut open a ring of bacterial DNA (a **plasmid**). The human DNA section is inserted into the plasmid.
3. The plasmid is inserted into a bacterium, which divides rapidly. As it divides, it copies the plasmid.
4. The bacteria, carrying instructions to make insulin, are **cultivated** on a large scale in **fermenters**.

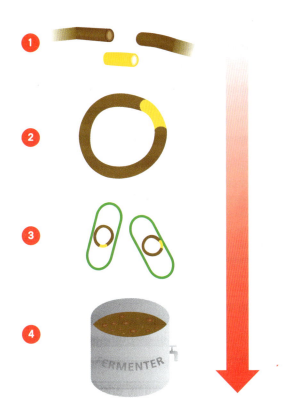

Fermentation

Fermentation is when microorganisms take food from their environment as an energy source and excrete waste substances like carbon dioxide. This changes the substances surrounding them.

A fermenter is a controlled environment that provides ideal conditions for the microorganisms to live, feed and produce the proteins needed.

HT A fermenter requires…
- **aseptic conditions** so the microorganisms aren't contaminated
- **nutrients** for the microorganisms to grow
- an **optimum temperature** for the microorganisms to grow
- the **correct pH** level
- **oxygenation** so the microorganisms can respire
- **agitation** (stirring) to keep the microorganisms in suspension and maintain an even temperature
- a **water-cooled jacket** to remove heat produced by the respiring microorganisms.

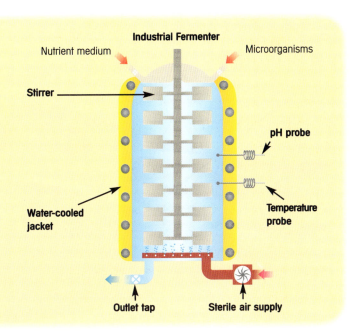

Industrial Fermenter

Nutrient medium

Microorganisms

Stirrer

pH probe

Water-cooled jacket

Temperature probe

Outlet tap

Sterile air supply

Inside Living Cells

Microorganisms and Food Production

Microorganisms can be used in some types of food production. For example…

- bacteria are used in the production of yoghurt
- **yeast** is used in the production of bread, beer and wine.

In the presence of oxygen, yeast converts glucose to water and carbon dioxide. In the absence of oxygen, it converts glucose to ethanol and carbon dioxide. This process is **fermentation**.

The advantages of using microorganisms to produce food are that they…

- grow and reproduce quickly
- are easy to handle and manipulate
- can be produced indoors (they're not dependent on climate)
- can make use of waste products from other industrial processes.

Aerobic Respiration

Aerobic respiration is a very efficient way of producing energy.

Ventilation (breathing in and out) supplies the oxygen needed for aerobic respiration.

Blood transports this **oxygen**, and **glucose**, to the body's cells. Enzymes in the cells cause the glucose and oxygen to react, producing **energy** that can be used for work, e.g. movement.

Glucose, oxygen and carbon dioxide move between the **capillaries** and respiring cells by **diffusion**:

- Glucose and oxygen diffuse from capillaries into respiring cells.
- Carbon dioxide diffuses from respiring cells into capillaries.

HT When muscle cells work hard (i.e. contract and relax a lot), their respiration rates increase as more energy is being used up.

More oxygen needs to be absorbed and more carbon dioxide needs to be removed. The gas exchange takes place by **diffusion** in the lungs at an increased rate.

A Working Muscle Cell

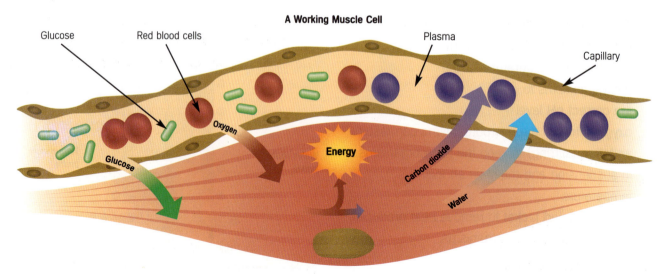

Glucose · Red blood cells · Plasma · Capillary · Oxygen · Glucose · Energy · Carbon dioxide · Water

Anaerobic Respiration

When you exercise, your **breathing rate** increases in order to get large amounts of oxygen into your body and larger amounts of carbon dioxide out. As these gases are transported by your blood, your **heart rate** increases to facilitate this.

During vigorous exercise, your lungs and bloodstream can't always deliver enough oxygen to your muscle cells to respire the glucose aerobically and meet the muscles' energy needs. When this happens, the glucose is only partly broken down. This means…

- only a small amount of energy is produced (about $\frac{1}{20}$ of the energy produced by aerobic respiration)
- most of the glucose is changed to lactic acid, a waste product.

This process is called anaerobic respiration.

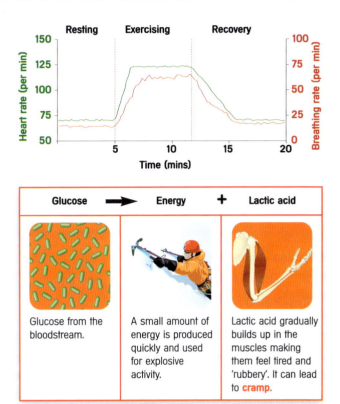

Glucose $\longrightarrow$	Energy $+$	Lactic acid
Glucose from the bloodstream.	A small amount of energy is produced quickly and used for explosive activity.	Lactic acid gradually builds up in the muscles making them feel tired and 'rubbery'. It can lead to cramp.

Oxygen Debt

The build up of **lactic acid** causes fatigue in the muscles and results in an **'oxygen debt'**, causing the muscles to stop contracting efficiently.

After exercise, lactic acid must be broken down quickly to avoid cell damage. Deep breathing provides enough oxygen to oxidise the lactic acid into carbon dioxide and water.

Monitoring Changes

Medical staff often need to monitor a patient's…
- temperature
- breathing rate
- heart rate.

This used to be done by observing the patient and checking their pulse rate at frequent intervals. Now, it's all done using digital thermometers and electronic breathing-rate and heart-rate monitors. This means that more reliable data can be collected (it's free from human error) and monitors can be left on constantly to provide a more accurate overall idea of the patient's health.

Because of advances in technology, this kind of equipment is now fairly cheap to produce so it's also being used by sports scientists and in gyms.

Key Words

Aerobic • Anaerobic • Capillary • Cramp • Diffusion • Glucose • Lactic acid • Microorganism • Respiration • Ventilation

Inside Living Cells

Keeping Healthy

In today's society, we're constantly bombarded with advice about what to eat and how much exercise to take to keep healthy.

Obesity is becoming more common in the UK, especially in young people. So, it's important to try to lead a **healthy lifestyle**.

Official **advice** about exercise and diet has changed over time because…

- our lifestyles have changed (e.g. cars mean we're less active so we use less energy)
- we know more about how the human body works and how certain foods affect us
- scientific research finds links between certain foods and health risks.

Exercise

Exercise is very important. You should exercise for about 20 minutes, four times a week, and aim to increase your heart rate by about 75%.

Sports like football and tennis increase your heart rate from about 72bpm (beats per minute) to 120bpm.

Diet

It's important to eat a **balanced diet** that includes all the basic food groups in the right proportions.

A balanced diet provides your body with the **energy** and nutrients it needs to work properly.

The amount of energy an individual needs depends on their lifestyle. For example, a builder would need more energy than an office worker. If you take in more energy through food and drink than you use (for growth, movement, etc.) you'll put on weight.

A number of special diets have recently been popular, such as low-carbohydrate diets. These **'fashionable diets'** may have a scientific basis but they're not healthy because they're not balanced. For example, a low-carbohydrate diet can lead to weight loss because carbohydrates are our main energy source. Without them, the body has to break down essential fat and protein stores for respiration.

Recommended Portions per Day

Fats, oils and sugar. Consume sparingly.

Dairy group. 2–3 servings.

Protein group. 2–3 servings.

Vegetable group. 3–5 servings.

Fruit group. 2–4 servings.

Carbohydrate group. 6–11 servings.

Glossary of Key Words

Adenine − one of four bases found in DNA; it pairs up with thymine.

Aerobic − with oxygen. Aerobic respiration uses oxygen to release energy and produce carbon dioxide and water.

Amino acid − a building block of a protein. Amino acids link up to form proteins.

Anaerobic − without oxygen. Anaerobic respiration is the incomplete breakdown of glucose to release a small amount of energy.

Bases − the four basic units of the genetic code: adenine, thymine, cytosine and guanine.

Capillary − the smallest of the body's blood vessels. Capillary walls are only one cell thick.

Coding − instructions for assembling amino acids to make proteins.

Cramp − muscular pain caused when muscles are overworked and lactic acid builds up. Muscles can't contract any more until lactic acid is removed.

Cultivated − growing and nurturing an organism, often to produce or enhance a particular feature.

Cytosine − one of four bases found in DNA; it pairs up with guanine.

Diffusion − the movement of a substance from a region of high concentration to a region of low concentration down a concentration gradient.

DNA (deoxyribonucleic acid) − the material found in chromosomes.

Double helix − the shape of a DNA molecule: two twisted strands linked by bases.

Fermentation − the process by which microorganisms obtain energy from a medium and produce other substances through respiration, changing the chemical composition of the medium. (When yeast does this, glucose is converted to carbon dioxide and alcohol.)

Fermenter − a container, a controlled environment for microorganisms to carry out fermentation.

Glucose − a simple sugar or carbohydrate; reacts with oxygen in the body to release energy.

Guanine − one of four bases found in DNA; it pairs up with cytosine.

Insulin − a hormone produced by the pancreas that controls blood sugar levels.

Lactic acid − produced by animal cells during anaerobic respiration.

Microorganism − an organism that can only be seen with a microscope (same as microbe).

Plasmid − circular DNA found in bacteria.

Protein − a food group; proteins are made up of long chains of amino acids.

Respiration − the process by which energy is released from glucose.

Strand − a single strand of the double-stranded DNA.

Thymine − one of four bases found in DNA; it pairs up with adenine.

Ventilation − breathing in and out.

HT Aseptic − sterile; free from contamination.

Messenger RNA (mRNA) − takes a copy of the DNA code from the nucleus to the cytoplasm.

Organelle − any specialised structure that's found inside a cell, e.g. the nucleus, ribosomes.

Polypeptide − a single-chain molecule of amino acids joined together by peptide bonds, e.g. protein.

Ribosome − an organelle involved in protein synthesis.

RNA (ribonucleic acid) − a single-stranded molecule containing the four bases. It is involved in protein synthesis.

Ribosomal RNA (rRNA) − RNA found in ribosomes.

Transcription − the process of making a strand of RNA from a single strand of DNA.

Transfer RNA (tRNA) − a single strand of RNA that carries specific amino acids to the ribosome for protein synthesis.

Translation − second phase of protein synthesis during which the protein chain (polypeptide) is produced.

Triplet − a sequence of three bases in a gene that codes for a single amino acid.

1 Which of the following statements apply to normal human body cells? Tick the correct options.

A   Contain one set of chromosomes ☐

B   Contain two sets of chromosomes ☐

C   Contain 46 chromosomes ☐

D   Contain 46 pairs of chromosomes ☐

HT

2 There are five stages in protein synthesis. Number the following stages **1–5** to put them into the correct order.

A   Amino acids are brought to the ribosome by tRNA. ☐

B   mRNA is made from a copy of the coding strand of DNA. ☐

C   DNA unravels at a specific gene. ☐

D   The triplet code is interpreted by a ribosome. ☐

E   mRNA moves from the nucleus to the cytoplasm. ☐

3 Draw lines between the boxes to match each word with its description.

mRNA	Chemical found in the nucleus of a cell
RNA	Carries specific amino acids to the ribosome
rRNA	Takes a copy of the genetic code to the cytoplasm
tRNA	Found in ribosomes
DNA	A single-stranded molecule involved in protein synthesis

4 Describe how insulin is made by genetic engineering.

....

....

....

HT

5 A fermenter is a controlled environment used to grow microorganisms. List five things that need to be controlled in a fermenter.

a) .... b) ....

c) .... d) ....

e) ....

6 Which of the following is not an advantage of using microbes in the production of food? Tick the correct option.

A They grow quickly ◯

B They reproduce quickly ◯

C They are easy to handle and manipulate ◯

D They are very small ◯

7 Aerobic respiration is an efficient way of releasing energy from food. Fill in the missing words to complete these sentences about aerobic respiration.

Blood transports .... and .... to the ....

of the body. .... in the cells make the glucose and oxygen react to release

.... that can be used to do work.

8 What is the main difference between aerobic respiration and anaerobic respiration?

....

....

....

9 What is obesity?

....

10 Explain what a balanced diet is.

....

....

Divide & Develop

Mitosis

Mitosis is the division of a cell nucleus to produce **two cell nuclei** that have **genetically identical** sets of **chromosomes**.

Mitosis occurs in order to produce new cells for growth and for the replacement of tissues.

1. A normal body cell nucleus has two sets of chromosomes.
2. Each chromosome copies itself.
3. The copies separate and the cell divides.
4. Each new cell has two sets of chromosomes and the same **genes** as the original cell.

Mitosis

HT Meiosis

Meiosis is when a **diploid** nucleus divides twice to produce four **haploid** nuclei. A diploid nucleus has **two sets** of chromosomes (e.g. a human body cell, which has 46 chromosomes in 23 pairs). A haploid nucleus has **one set** of chromosomes (e.g. a human sex cell, which has 23 chromosomes).

Meiosis produces cells that have genetically different sets of chromosomes. It occurs in sexually reproducing organisms to produce **gametes** (sex cells).

1. Cell with a diploid nucleus.
2. Each chromosome in the nucleus copies itself.
3. The chromosomes move to opposite sides of the cell with their copies.
4. The cell divides to produce two diploid cells.
5. The copies separate and move again.
6. The cells divide to produce four haploid nuclei.

	Mitosis	Meiosis
Where it happens	In most parts of the body	In the ovaries and testes
Number of cells made	Two cells	Four cells
Genetic variation	All cells are genetically identical	All cells are genetically different
Number of chromosomes in the nucleus	Two sets of chromosomes – diploid	One set of chromosomes – haploid
Purpose	Growth and cell replacement	Production of gametes

Meiosis

Growth

Growth is a permanent increase in the size of an organism.

There are three stages that contribute to the growth and development of organisms:

1 **Cell division** (mitosis) is the process where two cells are formed from one cell.

2 **Cell expansion** (**elongation**) is the process where cells (mainly in plants) elongate. The cells get bigger, rather than reproducing.

3 **Cell specialisation** is the process where an unspecialised (undifferentiated) cell becomes a specific type of cell.

Plant and Animal Growth

Plants and animals grow in different ways. Plants grow in height and width throughout their lives.

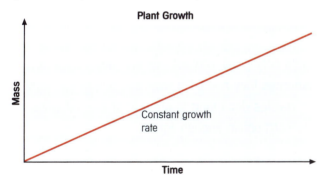

Most animals grow quickly at first, before slowing down and eventually stopping.

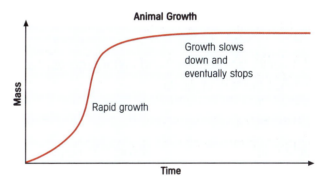

Measuring Growth

Length (height) is often used to measure growth in plants and humans. But it isn't a very accurate measure because it doesn't take into account growth in other directions, e.g. an increase in width. It's better to find the **total mass** (wet mass) of an organism.

Measuring the **dry mass** is the most accurate method. But this can only be done when the organism is dead, because it involves heating the organism to evaporate all the water in it and measuring the mass of what is left. So, wet mass is usually used. This means measuring the total mass of a living organism.

Key Words

Cell division • Chromosome • Diploid • Elongation • Gene • Growth • Haploid • Meiosis • Mitosis • Nucleus

Divide & Develop

Nature and Nurture

Nature and **nurture** are the factors that can influence the growth of an organism. Nature refers to the genes inherited from parents. Nurture refers to environmental influences. For example, there's a limit to how large an organism can grow, but individuals of that **species** will vary in size within these limits.

Height is a **continuous variable**; it has **continuous variation** (i.e. it can take any value in a range) rather than **discontinuous variation**. In humans, height is influenced by three factors:

- **Genes** – tall parents are likely to have tall children.
- **Hormones** – they coordinate growth in the body.
- **Nutrition** – a healthy, balanced diet with all the essential **nutrients** will allow an individual to achieve their full height potential.

The graph shows how height can vary within a group of people of the same age.

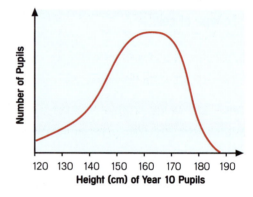

Growth and Distribution of Plants

Both nature (environment) and nurture (genes) can influence the size of plants.

Resource	How do plants get it?
Light – for photosynthesis	Absorb it through leaves
Carbon dioxide (CO_2) – for photosynthesis	Absorb it through leaves
Oxygen (O_2) – for respiration	Absorb it through leaves
Nutrients (nitrates and phosphates) – for growth and development	Absorb them from soil through roots
Temperature (warmth) – drives the plant's metabolism	From the surrounding environment

Plants only grow in places where they can get the **resources** they need. For example, this graph shows that daisies don't tend to grow in shade, because they can't obtain enough light.

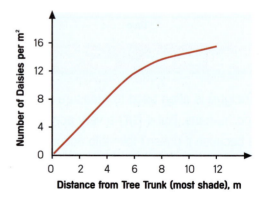

Plants also need hormones, to make their roots grow down into the soil and their shoots grow up into the air, an example of **phototropism**. People sometimes use **artificial hormones** to help plants grow.

Plant Hormones

Auxins are naturally occurring plant hormones that control cell growth and specialisation.

Plant growers use **synthetic auxin** sprays on their plants to ensure that fruit grows all year round. This means the plants produce fruit without fertilisation occurring, so the fruits don't contain seeds (pips).

Ethene is a plant hormone used to ripen fruit. For example, bananas are picked when they're unripe, and ethene is used to ripen them during transportation so they're ripe when they get to the shops.

Performance-Enhancing Drugs

Some drugs exist that act on the body in a similar way to natural growth hormones. In sports, these drugs are known as **performance-enhancing drugs** because they can…

* increase body mass and strength
* potentially improve performance.

Performance-enhancing drugs are banned in all sports as their use doesn't represent the athlete's true ability, which makes the competition unfair.

But, some athletes risk using them for a number of reasons, such as to…

* recover from an injury more quickly
* mask pain so that they can carry on performing
* be the best and win at all costs
* improve on their natural ability
* reap the financial rewards (cash prizes, sponsorship deals, etc.).

Anabolic Steroids

Anabolic **steroids** are performance-enhancing drugs that stimulate the development of muscle in a similar way to the male hormone testosterone.

But there are many health problems linked with anabolic steroids, including…

* liver disorders
* heart disease
* low **sperm** count in males (sometimes leading to sterility)
* personality changes, e.g. increased aggression.

Key Words

Auxins • Continuous variation •
Discontinuous variation • Hormone •
Nutrient • Phototropism • Species •
Sperm • Steroid

Divide & Develop

Regeneration

Plants can **regenerate** (grow) new leaves and branches if old ones are lost. But, very few animals can regenerate body parts.

Animals that can regenerate body parts tend to do so as a defence mechanism: they can sacrifice certain parts to escape capture by a predator. The table shows some examples of animals that can regenerate body parts.

Studying regeneration helps scientists to understand more about stem cells and how they could be used in medicine.

If cut in half, each half of a **worm** can regenerate the missing half.	
Young **spiders** can re-grow legs when they shed their skin (but adult spiders can't regenerate body parts).	
Many **reptiles** can shed their tails and even legs, and then re-grow them.	

Stem Cells

Most cells are **specialised** to perform a particular job efficiently. They become specialised by **differentiation**.

Plant cells can differentiate any time but animal cells only differentiate soon after they're made.

Stem cells are cells that are undifferentiated – they're unspecialised. In theory, this means they could differentiate into any type of cell. Research has shown that stem cells could potentially be used to replace damaged cells and tissues to help in the treatment of diseases. In an animal **embryo**, stem cells can differentiate into all other types of cells. But as the cells mature they lose this ability to change.

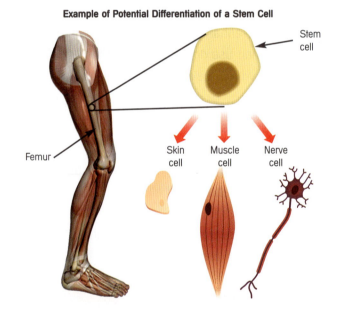

Example of Potential Differentiation of a Stem Cell

Stem cell

Femur

Skin cell   Muscle cell   Nerve cell

ⒽⓉ The Hayflick Limit

In 1965, Dr Leonard Hayflick discovered a limit to how many times a specialised cell can divide by mitosis. This is known as the **Hayflick limit**.

In human cells the Hayflick limit is about 52 divisions. As cells approach this limit, they start to show signs of old age.

Stem cells don't have a Hayflick limit: they divide throughout the organism's life. This means doctors could potentially produce lots of specialised cells from just a few stem cells. **Cancer cells** also don't have a Hayflick limit so all the cancer cells must be eliminated to treat the patient. This is why an early diagnosis is important.

Divide & Develop

Selective Breeding

To make a profit, a farmer's animals and crops must be efficient at producing food. This means using **selective breeding** (artificial selection) to produce high quality food, etc. **Pedigree analysis** is used to identify organisms to breed from. For example…

- **improving quality** – Jersey cows are selectively bred to produce rich, creamy milk that can be sold at a higher price than normal milk
- **increasing quantity** – sheep that produce twins are desirable as the farmer gets more animals, so these sheep are selectively bred
- **increasing yield** – dwarf wheat plants are selectively bred to produce high yielding seed-heads to maximise cost-effectiveness.

Key Words

Cancer cell • Differentiation • Embryo • Fetus • Nuclear transfer • Ovum • Pedigree analysis • Regeneration • Selective breeding • Stem cell

HT Cloning

It's now possible to **clone** mammals:

1. The **diploid** nucleus is taken from a mature body cell of the donor animal.
2. The nucleus is inserted into an empty **ovum**. This is **nuclear transfer**.
3. The egg cell is stimulated so it starts to divide by mitosis.
4. The resulting embryo is placed in the uterus of a surrogate mother.
5. The embryo develops into a **fetus** and is born.

In 1996, Dolly the sheep was cloned by this method. Sheep normally live for about 16 years, but Dolly was put down aged 6, as she had arthritis and lung disease – conditions usually suffered by older sheep. Defects in DNA are more likely to affect the organisation of cells and tissues during the development of cloned embryos, as the egg cell only gets genetic information from one parent. Scientists are concerned that cloning can lead to premature ageing and abnormalities (e.g. in brain structure). Research also suggests there are risks with the later stages of embryonic development of clones. Many don't even survive until birth.

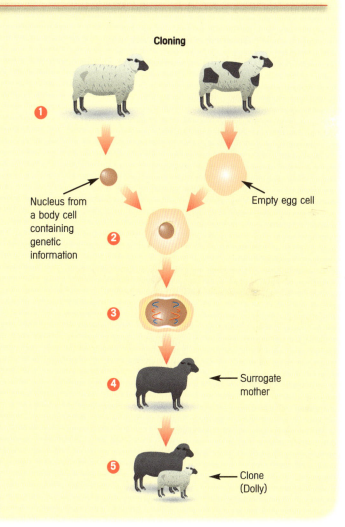

Divide & Develop

The Genetics Debate

Scientists have made great advances in understanding genes, chromosomes and **inheritance**. We now know…

- genes control characteristics
- genes are inherited
- whether an individual's genes put them at a higher risk of getting certain illnesses.

It might soon be possible to remove 'faulty' genes that cause genetic disorders. But there are concerns about the **ethical issues** of this. For example…

- parents could start selecting the characteristics of their offspring, leading to '**designer babies**'
- there may be an increase in abortion rates
- insurance companies might refuse to cover people with an increased risk of genetic disease.

Gene Therapy

Gene therapy is an experimental technique. It involves the **genetic modification** of cells by transplanting genes (DNA) into an individual's cells to treat inherited conditions. But the genes are transferred into body cells, not **gametes** (sex cells), so they can't be passed on to the offspring.

At the moment, gene therapy can only provide short-term relief from the symptoms of the disease.

HT Potentially, gene therapy could be used to treat diseases like **cancer**, by inserting missing genes or replacing damaged genes.

Scientists are researching the possibility of…

- introducing genes that will improve patients' immune response to diseases
- injecting cancer cells with genes that make them more sensitive to treatment
- introducing genes that make healthy cells more resistant to high doses of anti-cancer drugs
- injecting cancer cells with genes that can destroy them.

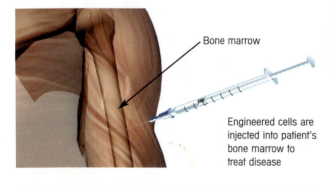

Bone marrow

Engineered cells are injected into patient's bone marrow to treat disease

Legal Terminations

In humans, pregnancy lasts an average of 40 weeks. The legal time limit for a **termination** (**abortion**) is 24 weeks into the pregnancy. This limit is based on the survival chances of the fetus if it was born prematurely. A 24-week old fetus would be very unlikely to survive.

But, some people want the limit reduced to 18 weeks. They argue that a 24-week old fetus can feel pain and respond to sound.

They say that most of its body systems are functional and its brain is growing quickly. Other people think abortion should be made illegal altogether.

Key Words

Gametes • Genetic modification • Inheritance • Termination

Divide & Develop

Glossary of Key Words

Auxins – plant growth hormones.

Cell division – the splitting of a cell to produce new cells.

Chromosome – a long strand of genes made from DNA.

Continuous variation – variation in a feature that can take any number of values within a range.

Differentiation – the process by which a cell becomes specialised to perform a specific function.

Discontinuous variation – variation in a feature that can only have a set number of values.

Elongation – when a plant becomes longer during the process of differentiation.

Embryo – a growing cluster of cells; the first stage in the development of a baby.

Gametes – sex cells, i.e. the eggs (ova) and sperms.

Gene – a section of DNA that controls a particular feature.

Genetic modification – altering the natural genetic make-up of an organism.

Growth – the permanent increase in the size of an organism.

Hormones – chemical messengers produced by the endocrine glands and transported by the blood to target organs or cells.

Inheritance – the process by which characteristics are passed on from one generation to the next.

Mitosis – a type of cell division in a cell's nucleus that produces diploid cells for growth or to replace damaged, worn out cells.

Nucleus – the part of a cell that contains chromosomes.

Nutrient – a chemical compound needed by living organisms for the healthy production of new cells.

Pedigree analysis – tracing patterns of inheritance through several generations.

Phototropism – a plant growth response to light (shoots and stems grow towards the light).

Regeneration – the replacement of body parts by growing new ones.

Selective breeding – the artificial selection of individual organisms for breeding, based on their desirable characteristics.

Species – a group of organisms that can breed and produce fertile offspring.

Sperm – the male sex cell.

Stem cell – an undifferentiated cell that has the potential to develop into a specialised cell.

Steroids – drugs made up of hormones.

Termination – bringing to an end, as in abortion (ending) of a pregnancy.

HT **Cancer cell** – a cell that divides uncontrollably to eventually form a tumour.

Diploid – a cell nucleus that contains two sets of chromosomes; a normal body cell nucleus.

Fetus – the development from an embryo, usually about seven weeks after fertilisation.

Haploid – a cell nucleus that contains one set of chromosomes; the sex cells.

Meiosis – a type of division of a cell's nucleus that produces haploid cells (gametes).

Nuclear transfer – the process where a donor nucleus is transferred into an empty egg cell.

Ovum (plural: ova) – an egg cell; the female sex cell.

Practice Questions

1 Mitosis and meiosis are types of nuclear division. Complete this table to summarise the differences between mitosis and meiosis.

	Meiosis	Mitosis
Where it takes place	In the testes and ovaries	a) ....
Number of cells made	b)	Two cells
Genetic variation	c)	Genetically identical
Number of chromosomes in the nucleus	One set per nucleus	d) ....
Its purpose	Gamete production	e) ....

2 Number the following statements **1–4** to show the correct order in which mitosis takes place.

A Each chromosome copies itself.

B Each new cell has two sets of chromosomes.

C A normal body cell has two sets of chromosomes.

D The two copies of chromosomes separate and the cell divides.

3 Draw lines between the boxes to match each word with its correct definition.

Chromosome	A section of DNA that controls a feature
Diploid	A long strand of DNA
Gene	A type of cell division
Haploid	A cell nucleus with two sets of chromosomes
Mitosis	A cell nucleus with one set of chromosomes

4 Explain the difference between cell division and cell expansion.

....

....

5 List the three factors that affect a person's height.

a) ....   b) ....   c) ....

6 What effect do performance-enhancing drugs have on the body?

....

7 a) Stem cells are said to be **undifferentiated**. What does this mean?

....

HT b) Stem cells don't have a Hayflick limit. Explain what this means.

....

8 Which of the following is **not** usually a reason for using selective breeding? Tick the correct option.

A Improving quality ⬚   **B** Improving quantity ⬚

C Increasing yield ⬚   **D** Increasing volume of waste materials ⬚

HT

9 Dolly the sheep was the first successfully cloned mammal. Number the following statements **1–5** to put them into the correct order and describe how the cloning process works.

A The nucleus is inserted into an empty ovum cell. ⬚

B The embryo develops into a fetus. ⬚

C The diploid nucleus is taken from a mature body cell. ⬚

D The embryo is placed in the uterus of a surrogate mother. ⬚

E The egg cell is stimulated to divide by mitosis. ⬚

10 What are gametes? Tick the correct option.

A Body cells ⬚   **B** Genetically modified cells ⬚

C Sex cells ⬚   **D** Transgenic cells ⬚

HT

11 Gene therapy is a new technique that involves genes being transplanted. Potentially it could be used to treat diseases. List two possible uses of gene therapy that scientists are researching.

a) ....

b) ....

Energy Flow

Biospheres

The **biosphere** is the part of the Earth and its atmosphere where life exists.

Scientists can build artificial biospheres – structures designed to sustain life in a place that otherwise wouldn't have life. Some scientists think that an artificial biosphere on another planet (e.g. Mars) would be a way to colonise the planet. The biosphere would have to be self-contained and **sustainable**. It would need…

- photosynthesising plants to supply oxygen and food
- the ability to recycle all waste materials
- a method of keeping warm
- a way to melt Martian ice.

Plant and Animal Cells

All living organisms are made of cells. The structures of different cells are related to their function. Both **plant cells** and **animal cells** have a **nucleus**, **cytoplasm** and cell **membrane**. In addition…

- all plant cells have a **cellulose cell wall**
- most plant cells have a **vacuole**
- plants that are exposed to light have **chloroplasts** containing **chlorophyll** (green pigments) in their cells.

Specialised plant cells: **xylem** cells transport water and minerals from the roots to where they're needed; **phloem** cells transport food in solution from the leaves to where it's needed, or for storage.

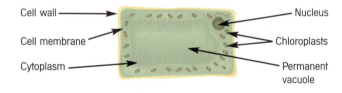

A Palisade Cell from a Leaf

Cell wall — Nucleus
Cell membrane — Chloroplasts
Cytoplasm — Permanent vacuole

A Cheek Cell from a Human

Nucleus — Cytoplasm
Cell membrane

How Green Plants Make Food

Green plants make their own food by **photosynthesis**. It occurs in the chloroplasts of the many cells of green plants that are exposed to light.

Reactants	→	Products
Carbon dioxide + Water	$\xrightarrow[\text{Chlorophyll}]{\text{Light}}$	Glucose + Oxygen
$6CO_2$ + $6H_2O$	$\xrightarrow[\text{Chlorophyll}]{\text{Light}}$	$C_6H_{12}O_6$ + $6O_2$

Key Words

Active transport • Animal cell • Biosphere • Cellulose cell wall • Chlorophyll • Chloroplast • Cytoplasm • Membrane • Mineral salt • Nucleus • Osmosis • Phloem • Photosynthesis • Plant cell • Root • Sustainability • Vacuole • Xylem

Factors Affecting Photosynthesis

Temperature, carbon dioxide concentration and light intensity interact to affect the rate of photosynthesis. Any one could be the **limiting factor**. Look at the graphs.

As **temperature** rises, so does the rate of photosynthesis (❶). But, if the temperature goes above 37°C, the enzymes controlling photosynthesis are destroyed and the rate of photosynthesis drops to zero (❷).

As **carbon dioxide concentration** rises, so does the rate of photosynthesis (❶). But it only affects it up to a certain point. After that point, it's no longer the limiting factor: light or temperature must be (❷).

As **light intensity** increases, so does the rate of photosynthesis (❶). But it only affects it up to a certain point (❷). After that point, it's no longer the limiting factor: carbon dioxide or temperature must be.

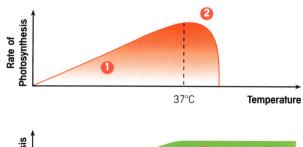

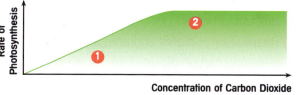

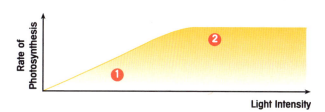

(HT) Absorbing Mineral Salts

Plants absorb water from the soil by **osmosis** through their root hairs. They also absorb **mineral salts** (or mineral ions) from the soil through their root hairs but because they absorb mineral salts against a concentration gradient, they use **active transport**. This means the plant must use **energy** from **respiration** to absorb mineral salts.

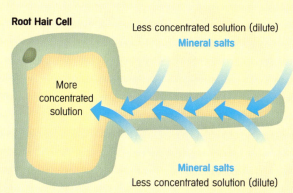

Root Hair Cell

Less concentrated solution (dilute)
Mineral salts

More concentrated solution

Mineral salts
Less concentrated solution (dilute)

Mineral	Why it is Needed	Result of Deficiency
Nitrogen	• To make proteins for growth	• Stunted growth
Phosphorus	• To make cell membranes • To make proteins	• Poor root growth
Potassium	• To help the enzymes involved in respiration and photosynthesis to work properly	• Yellow leaves with dead patches or leaves with yellow edges
Magnesium	• To make chlorophyll	• Yellow leaves

Uses for Plants

We use plants for all sorts of things. We use…

- **flowers** – for food (e.g. broccoli) and decorations (e.g. bunches of flowers)
- **roots** – for food (e.g. carrots, beetroot)

- **the stem** – for food (e.g. celery) and building materials (e.g. wood, bamboo)
- **leaves** – for food (e.g. lettuce) and building materials (e.g. roofs of huts in some countries).

Energy Flow

The Carbon Cycle

Carbon forms the basis of all living things. The constant cycling of carbon is called the **carbon cycle**.

There are four main processes in the carbon cycle:

1 **Photosynthesis** – green plants take in carbon dioxide from the atmosphere to produce **glucose**.

2 **Respiration** – plants and animals respire, releasing carbon dioxide into the atmosphere.

3 **Decay** – when plants and animals die, other animals and **microorganisms** feed on them and respire, breaking them down and releasing carbon dioxide into the air.

4 **Combustion** – fossil fuels are burned, releasing carbon dioxide into the air.

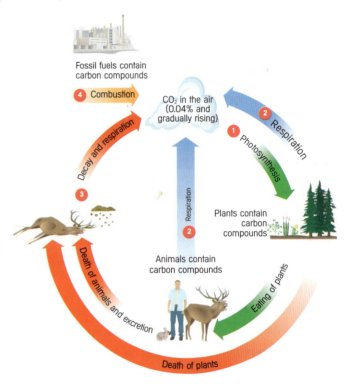

The Nitrogen Cycle

Nitrogen is a vital element of all living things. It's used to make proteins needed for plant and animal growth. The **nitrogen cycle** shows how nitrogen and its compounds are cycled. **Bacteria** play an important role in the nitrogen cycle.

There are five main processes in the nitrogen cycle:

1 **Nitrogen-fixing bacteria** in the soil or roots of leguminous plants convert atmospheric nitrogen into nitrates.

2 When plants are eaten, nitrogen is turned into animal protein.

3 Dead organisms and waste contain ammonium compounds. **Decomposers** convert urea, faeces and protein from dead organisms into ammonium compounds.

4 **Nitrifying bacteria** convert ammonium compounds into nitrates in the soil.

5 **Denitrifying bacteria** convert nitrates into atmospheric nitrogen and ammonium compounds.

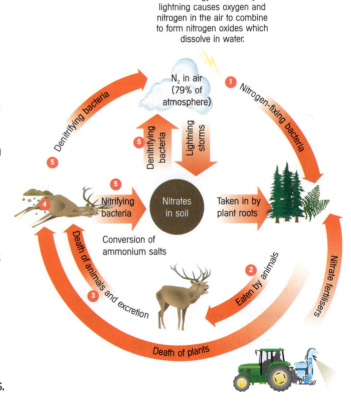

Nitrogenous Fertilisers

Plants need nitrogen for healthy growth but they can't use nitrogen from the air because it's inert and not all of them have nitrogen-fixing bacteria in their roots. Farmers use **fertilisers** to replace the nitrogen in the soil that's been used up by crops.

This means crop yields can be increased. But, indiscriminate or careless use of fertilisers can damage the environment and lead to **eutrophication** (as shown below).

Nitrates cause excessive algal growth, which blocks off sunlight to other plants

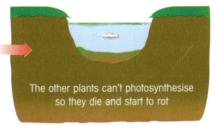

The other plants can't photosynthesise so they die and start to rot

The rotting process uses up oxygen and the water can't support life

The Greenhouse Effect

Carbon dioxide and methane are known as 'greenhouse gases' because they act as an insulating layer around the Earth.

They keep a lot of the heat from the Sun within the Earth's atmosphere. This is known as the **greenhouse effect**.

Global Warming

Levels of carbon dioxide and methane are increasing, so more heat is being kept inside the atmosphere.

This is leading to **global warming**.

- **Deforestation** reduces photosynthesis so less carbon dioxide is removed. It also reduces the amount of carbon dioxide locked up as wood.
- **Burning** of the chopped down wood, and from industry, produces carbon dioxide.
- Increased **microorganism activity** on decaying material produces carbon dioxide.
- **Rice fields** and **cattle** produce methane.

If the average temperature on Earth increases by just a few degrees, millions of people will be affected. There will be…

- substantial climate changes
- a rise in sea levels.

HT The human population is increasing and, as a result, levels of greenhouse gases are increasing.

Humans are using the Earth's resources **unsustainably** (i.e. with no consideration for future generations).

For example, human activities such as deforestation and the burning of fossil fuels have led to an increase in the amount of carbon dioxide being released into the atmosphere.

Key Words

Carbon cycle • Combustion • Decomposer • Deforestation • Denitrifying bacteria • Eutrophication • Fertiliser • Global warming • Glucose • Microorganism • Nitrifying bacteria • Nitrogen cycle • Nitrogen-fixing bacteria • Respiration

Energy Flow

Food Production and Distribution

Developed countries produce a lot of food. There's a constant, plentiful supply with competitive prices and lots of choice. But this can also be a problem. Many people eat too much food that has a high fat and / or salt content. This can lead to health problems such as **obesity**, heart **disease**, diabetes and arthritis.

Developing countries often don't have enough food. People suffer from **malnutrition** and problems such as reduced resistance to infection.

Hundreds of thousands of people in developing countries die from starvation every year. Solutions to the problem of unequal food distribution include…
- sending food from richer countries to poorer ones
- teaching people how to produce their own food.

But the costs of transporting food and keeping it fresh would be high, and the typically hot, dry conditions in developing countries often prevent food from growing there.

Maximising Food Production

Food production can be maximised by using designated food production plants like fish farms and large greenhouses.

These provide optimum feeding / growth conditions.

Key Words

Disease • Food production • Predator

HT Fish Farms

Fish farms consist of large cages suspended in the sea or lakes. The fish are encouraged to grow by…
- keeping eggs and young fish in tanks until they can fend for themselves
- providing a high-protein diet
- keeping **predators** away
- using chemicals to combat pests and **disease**.

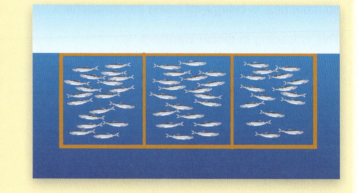

Greenhouses

The conditions in greenhouses can be controlled to provide optimum growing conditions:
- optimum light, temperature and carbon dioxide concentration for **photosynthesis**
- appropriate use of herbicides, pesticides and **fertilisers**
- plenty of water.

Glossary of Key Words

Animal cell – the basic structural and functional unit of animals.

Biosphere – the part of the Earth that supports life.

Carbon cycle – the process of carbon being recycled between living organisms and the environment.

Cellulose cell wall – a wall in a plant cell formed from a carbohydrate. It provides the cell with structural support.

Chlorophyll – green chemical found in chloroplasts, which absorbs light for photosynthesis.

Chloroplast – an organelle found in the green parts of plants; contains chlorophyll.

Combustion – the process by which fuel is burned to release heat energy (carbon dioxide is produced).

Cytoplasm – everything inside a cell that isn't the nucleus or other organelles.

Decomposer – organisms (typically bacteria and fungi) that break down dead animals and plants.

Deforestation – the cutting down of very large areas of forests (typically rainforests).

Denitrifying bacteria – bacteria that release nitrogen from compounds containing nitrogen.

Disease – an illness caused by a microorganism, environmental change or 'faulty' genes.

Eutrophication – the excessive growth and decay of aquatic plants due to increased levels of nutrients in the water that results in oxygen levels dropping so that fish and other animal populations die.

Fertiliser – a chemical that contains nitrates, phosphates and potassium. They're added to the soil to replace the minerals used up by plants.

Food production – the process by which food is cultivated or grown.

Global warming – the increase in the average temperature of the Earth, caused by a rise in the levels of greenhouse gases in the atmosphere.

Glucose – a carbohydrate, sometimes referred to as a simple sugar; a product of photosynthesis.

Membrane – surrounds cells and controls the movement of chemicals and particles into and out of the cell.

Microorganism – a microscopic organism (same as microbe).

Nitrifying bacteria – bacteria that convert ammonium compounds into nitrates.

Nitrogen cycle – the process of nitrogen being recycled between living organisms and the environment.

Nitrogen-fixing bacteria – bacteria that make nitrates from atmospheric nitrogen.

Nucleus – part of a cell that contains chromosomes.

Phloem – tissue that conducts nutrients round a plant.

Photosynthesis – the process by which green plants use light energy to make glucose.

Plant cell – the basic structural and functional unit of plants.

Respiration – a series of chemical reactions by which living organisms release energy from food.

Root – part of a plant that grows into the soil; absorbs water and minerals, and anchors the plant.

Sustainability – maintaining the environment, ecosystem, energy sources, etc. whilst developing.

Transpiration – the loss of water from plants, especially from their leaves.

Vacuole – a large space in the centre of a plant cell that is full of cell sap.

Xylem – tissue that transports water and mineral ions in a plant from the roots to the shoots.

HT **Active transport –** the process of using energy to move molecules against a concentration gradient (from low concentration to high concentration).

Mineral salts – chemicals needed by living organisms to live and stay healthy (also known as ions, mineral ions, salts and minerals).

Osmosis – the net movement of water particles from a dilute solution to a more concentrated solution across a selectively permeable membrane.

Predator – an animal that hunts, kills and eats prey.

Practice Questions

1 Which of the following structures are found in both plant and animal cells? Tick the correct options.

A Nucleus ☐

B Cell wall ☐

C Cytoplasm ☐

D Cell membrane ☐

E Chloroplasts ☐

2 The diagram shows a plant cell. Match labels **A**, **B** and **C** with the labels **1–3** on the diagram.

A Chloroplast ☐

B Cell wall ☐

C Vacuole ☐

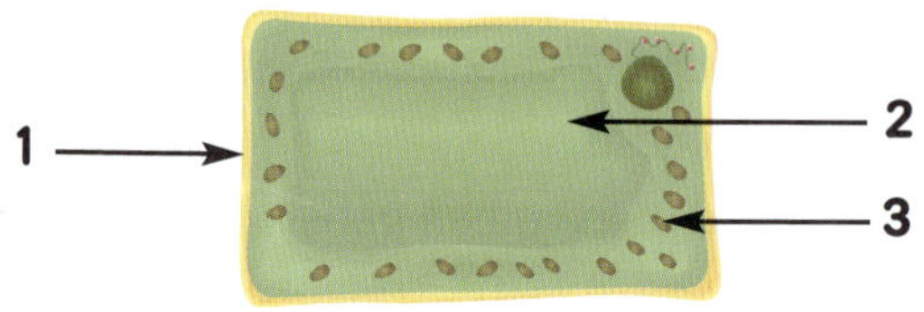

3 Which of the following is the process by which plants make food? Tick the correct option.

A Fermentation ☐

B Osmosis ☐

C Photosynthesis ☐

D Respiration ☐

4 Which of the following is **not** a limiting factor of photosynthesis? Tick the correct option.

A Temperature ☐

B Oxygen concentration ☐

C Carbon dioxide concentration ☐

D Light intensity ☐

HT

5 Which of the following is the correct definition of osmosis? Tick the correct option.

A The net movement of water molecules from a concentrated solution to a dilute solution across a selectively permeable membrane ☐

B The net movement of water molecules from a dilute solution to a more concentrated solution across a permeable membrane ☐

C The net movement of water molecules from a dilute solution to a more concentrated solution across a selectively permeable membrane ☐

D The net movement of a solution from a dilute solution to a more concentrated solution across a selectively permeable membrane ☐

Practice Questions

6 (Circle) the correct options in the following sentences, which describe the carbon cycle.

Respiration **releases / removes / takes in** carbon dioxide. Combustion releases **oxygen / carbon dioxide / nitrogen**. Decay releases carbon dioxide. Photosynthesis **releases / removes / takes in** carbon dioxide.

7 Fill in the missing words to complete the following sentences about the nitrogen cycle.

a) Nitrogen-fixing bacteria are found in .... and root nodules. They convert

nitrogen to ....

b) .... convert urea, faeces and protein into ammonium compounds.

c) Denitrifying bacteria are found in the soil. They convert nitrates into atmospheric ....

and .... compounds.

8 Explain how nitrogenous fertilisers contribute to eutrophication.

....

....

....

9 Explain how the greenhouse effect leads to global warming.

....

....

....

HT

10 Explain how farming fish encourages fish growth.

....

....

11 How do greenhouses provide good conditions for growing plants?

....

....

Interdependence

Interdependence and Competition

Interdependence refers to a relationship between living **organisms** where they depend on each other for a resource or for survival. What happens to one organism affects what happens to the others: they're **dependent** on each other.

There's always **competition** between individuals and species when they need the same **resources** to survive.

Plants need…
- space for their leaves to absorb sunlight (for photosynthesis)
- water and minerals from the soil.

Animals need…
- space to breed and build a home, and territory for hunting
- food and water.

Predation

During **predation**, there's a cycle between the number of **predators** and the number of **prey**:
- When the prey **population** is large, the predator population increases.
- Lots of prey are eaten so their numbers fall.
- The predator population then falls as well.

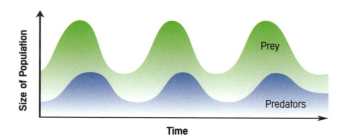

Adaptation

Adaptations are features or behaviours that make an organism well-suited to its **environment**.

Adaptations develop as the result of **evolution**. They increase an organism's chance of survival.

Examples of Adaptations

Polar bears have adapted to a cold **terrestrial** climate. They have…
- a lot of insulating fat and a small surface area to volume ratio to reduce heat loss
- large feet to spread their weight on the ice
- powerful legs to swim and catch food
- a whitish coat for camouflage.

Camels have adapted to a hot terrestrial climate and…
- have a large surface area to volume ratio to increase heat loss
- have almost no body fat beneath their skin
- lose very little water through urine / sweating
- can drink up to 20 gallons of water at once.

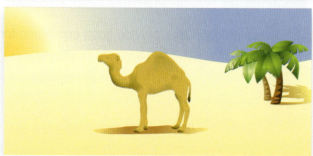

Examples of Adaptations (Cont.)

Fish have adapted to an **aquatic** environment. They have…

- a streamlined shape to travel through water
- gills that have a large surface area to obtain as much dissolved oxygen as possible from the water.

Cacti have adapted to a hot terrestrial climate. They have…

- a thick waxy surface to reduce water loss
- spines to protect against predators
- stomata that only open at night to reduce water loss
- either shallow roots to absorb surface water or deep roots to tap into underground supplies.

Extreme Habitats

Organisms living in **extreme environments** need very special adaptations to be able to survive.

In the **Antarctic**, temperatures can go below -50°C. Penguins have adapted to live in these conditions because they…

- have a compact shape, so not much heat is lost through the surface
- have thick layers of insulating fat under the skin
- have very tightly packed, waterproof feathers
- huddle in large, tightly packed groups called rookeries: they constantly move into the centre so those on the outside don't get too cold.

Hydrothermal vents (deep sea volcanic vents) are found under the sea and discharge water at 400°C and above. There are no photosynthesising plants here as it's completely dark. But some organisms have adapted to live in these conditions by…

- being able to cope with high temperature and high pressure
- having very highly developed senses other than sight.

Conditions at **high altitudes** (e.g. mountain tops) are cold and windy with a shortage of oxygen.

The density of air decreases the higher you go, so people have to acclimatise by spending time at progressively higher altitudes.

This lets the body produce extra red blood cells to capture as much oxygen as possible to transport around the body.

Key Words

Adaptation • Aquatic • Competition • Environment • Extreme environment • Hydrothermal vent • Interdependence • Organism • Population • Predation • Resource • Terrestrial

Interdependence

Pollution

Pollution is the contamination of the environment by waste substances that are produced as the result of human activity.

Many waste substances are formed from the burning of fossil fuels to release energy.

Air Pollution

Air pollution may consist of…

- **hydrocarbons** – released from the combustion of fossil fuels
- **carbon dioxide** – an important greenhouse gas released from the combustion of fossil fuels
- **sulphur dioxide** – released from the combustion of fossil fuels and a contributor to acid rain
- **carbon monoxide** – released from vehicle exhausts and from many heavy industries.

Water Pollution

Water pollution may consist of…

- **sewage** (human waste) – bacteria feed on it and use up the oxygen in the water, causing other water plants and fish to die of asphyxiation (lack of oxygen)
- **nitrates** – found in **fertilisers**, nitrates are washed out of soil into streams, rivers, etc. They cause water plants to grow excessively, and when they die, bacteria feed on them, using up the oxygen in the water and causing other water plants and fish to die
- **phosphates** – found in waste water from laundries, run-off from fields, and in fertilisers, phosphates can have the same effect as nitrates.

All these types of pollution can cause **eutrophication**.

Key Words

Indicator • Nitrates • Phosphates • Pollution • Population • Sewage

Effects of Human Activity

Differing economical and industrial conditions influence and direct how **human activity** affects the environment and can change **population** sizes all over the world. These human activities include:

- **Land use** – for building houses, roads, factories, etc., for quarrying, and for farming, which often uses fertilisers and pesticides.
- **Raw materials** such as natural gas, crude oil, coal and metal ores are used by humans.
- Humans produce **waste** in the form of **pollution** (in the air, on land and in water), and pile up waste to create large landfill sites.

All these activities have the effect of…

- changing natural habitats
- reducing the numbers of naturally occurring populations.

Developed, highly industrialised countries actually produce less air pollution overall than industrially developing countries. This is because developed countries have enforced guidelines and regulations for harmful emissions over the last few decades. But the increase in levels of air pollution in developing countries is the result of recent industrial development and economic growth, e.g. China.

Environmental Change

It's important to protect natural habitats in order to protect the populations that live there.

Pollution changes habitats so populations either move away or die.

Over such a short timescale, they can't **evolve** to cope with the changes. So, to prevent species becoming **endangered**, or even **extinct**, it's vital to protect their environment.

Air Pollution Indicators

Lichens are sensitive to sulphur dioxide air pollution and even quite low levels can kill them. So they are **indicators** of air pollution.

This table shows some data collected from a city polluted by sulphur dioxide. It shows that the more air pollution there is, the fewer lichens there are.

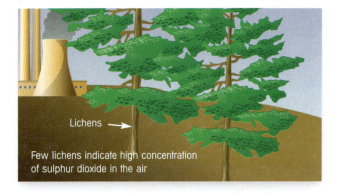

Lichens →

Few lichens indicate high concentration of sulphur dioxide in the air

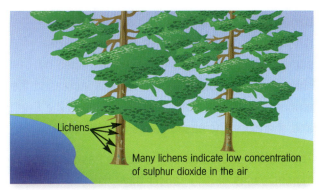

Lichens →

Many lichens indicate low concentration of sulphur dioxide in the air

Distance from City Centre	Number of Different Lichen Species	Sulphur Dioxide Levels (Arbitrary Units)
0	0	210
2	1	144
4	4	91
6	8	47
8	12	10

Interdependence

Conservation and Recycling

Conservation keeps ecosystems stable as environmental conditions change. These conditions include…
- **biotic** factors (living things)
- **abiotic** factors (temperature, humidity, etc.).

Conservation can lead to greater **biodiversity** by…
- preventing species from becoming extinct
- maintaining variation within species
- preserving habitats.

Conservation management techniques include…
- **reforestation** – the planting of forests on barren areas of land to provide new habitats
- **coppicing** – cutting down young trees just above ground level to encourage side shoots to grow; the process is repeated every few years
- **replacement planting** – planting trees to replace those cut down and maintain habitats.

Recycling is an important part of sustainable development. Local councils encourage us to recycle materials such as paper, plastic, metal and glass. They also encourage us to use compost heaps and bins for **biodegradable** items.

Recycling reduces demand for raw materials and reduces the problem of **waste disposal.**

Key Words

Biodegradable • Biodiversity • Chlorofluorocarbons • Conservation • Coppicing • Global temperature • Greenhouse gases • Ozone • Recycling • Reforestation • Replacement planting • Skin cancer • Waste disposal

Global Temperature

The average (mean) **global temperature** has increased over the last two centuries due to an increase in **greenhouse gases** in the atmosphere.

This is known as **global warming**.

HT Global warming will cause flooding, changes in weather patterns and droughts.

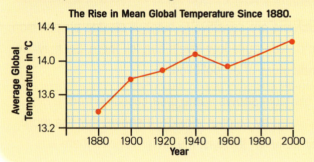

The Rise in Mean Global Temperature Since 1880.

The Ozone Layer and Skin Cancer

Ozone filters out some of the harmful ultraviolet (UV) radiation that can cause **skin cancer**. But some of the ozone layer has been damaged by **chlorofluorocarbons** (CFCs). This has increased the amount of UV light reaching the surface of the Earth and, therefore, increased cases of skin cancer.

The graphs show that as the ozone has become thinner, cases of skin cancer have risen.

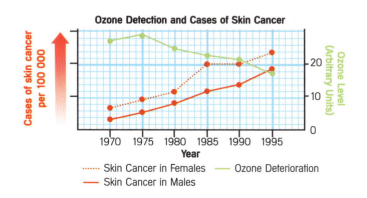

Ozone Detection and Cases of Skin Cancer

· · · · · Skin Cancer in Females   —— Ozone Deterioration
—— Skin Cancer in Males

Interdependence

Glossary of Key Words

Adaptation – a feature or type of behaviour that makes an organism better suited to survive in its habitat.

Aquatic – in water, e.g. a river habitat.

Biodegradable – materials that decompose by the action of microorganisms.

Biodiversity – the variety of different types of organisms in a habitat or ecosystem.

Chlorofluorocarbons (CFCs) – chemicals that used to be frequently used in solvents; they damage the ozone layer.

Competition – the rivalry between members of the same species, or members of different species, for a resource that they both need.

Conservation – the process by which ecosystems are kept stable as environmental conditions (both biotic and abiotic) change.

Coppicing – cutting down young trees to just above ground level to encourage the growth of side shoots; the process is repeated every few years.

Environment – the surroundings in which an organism lives.

Extreme environment – a place where the living conditions for organisms are particularly harsh, e.g. the Antarctic (extreme cold).

Global temperature – the mean temperature of the Earth (taking into account the high temperatures in the tropics and the extremely low temperatures of the Polar regions).

Greenhouse gases – gases in the Earth's atmosphere that absorb radiation and stop it from leaving the Earth's atmosphere, e.g. carbon dioxide and methane.

Hydrothermal vents – deep sea volcanic vents that release very hot liquids.

Indicators – organisms that can indicate the presence or lack of something, e.g. pollution.

Interdependence – the relationship between organisms where one organism depends on another for a resource.

Nitrates – an important source of nitrogen for plants; nitrates are absorbed from the soil by the roots; constituent of many fertilisers, needed for healthy growth.

Organism – a living thing.

Ozone – a layer of gas in the upper atmosphere that protects us from harmful UV rays by absorbing them.

Phosphates – an important source of phosphorus for plants; phosphates are absorbed from the soil by the roots; constituent of many fertilisers, needed for healthy growth.

Pollution – the contamination of an environment by chemicals, waste or heat that threatens existing habitats and / or endangers organisms.

Population – a group of organisms of the same species living in a defined area.

Predation – the process of predators hunting for prey.

Recycling – the process by which resources are used again.

Reforestation – the planting of forests.

Replacement planting – the planting of trees to replace those cut down.

Resource – a raw material that is used by an organism.

Sewage – human waste consisting of faeces and urine together with toilet paper and sanitary products, which are flushed down toilets.

Skin cancer – a disease that causes cells in the skin to divide uncontrollably to form tumours.

Terrestrial – on (dry) land, i.e. a land habitat.

Waste disposal – the removal of rubbish.

Practice Questions

1 Organisms have to be adapted in order to survive.

    a) Suggest three ways, with explanations, in which the polar bear is adapted to survive in the Arctic.

        i) ....

        ii) ....

        iii) ....

    b) Suggest three ways, with explanations, in which the camel is adapted to life in the desert.

        i) ....

        ii) ....

        iii) ....

2 Draw lines between the boxes to match each word with its correct definition.

Interdependence	A group of organisms of the same species
Competition	Something that is used by an organism
Resource	The process of predators hunting their prey
Predation	The relationship between organisms where one organism depends on another for a resource
Population	Rivalry between organisms for a resource that they both need
Adaptation	Something that makes an organism better able to survive

3 Explain why mammals that live at high altitudes have extra red blood cells.

....

....

....

4 What is meant by the term 'pollution'?

....

....

5 Which one of the following does **not** pollute the air? Tick the correct option.

A Carbon dioxide ☐

B Sulphur dioxide ☐

C Carbon monoxide ☐

D Oxygen ☐

6 Which substances / chemicals often contribute to the eutrophication of water? Tick the correct options.

A Sewage ☐

B Nitrates ☐

C Oxygen ☐

D Carbon dioxide ☐

E Phosphates ☐

F Hydrocarbons ☐

7 Explain how environmental change can lead to the extinction of a species.

....

....

....

8 Why are lichens used as indicators of sulphur dioxide pollution?

....

....

HT

9 List three things that are likely to happen as the result of global warming.

a) .... b) .... c) ....

10 How do chlorofluorocarbons (CFCs) contribute to skin cancer?

....

....

Synthesis

Balancing Equations

In all chemical reactions the **mass of the reactants is equal to the mass of the products**. This means that there must be the same number of atoms on both sides of the equation.

Number of atoms in reactants	=	Number of atoms in products

Writing Balanced Equations

Follow these steps to write a balanced equation:

1 Write a word equation	Calcium carbonate	+	Hydrochloric acid	→	Calcium chloride	+ Carbon dioxide + Water
2 Substitute in formulae	$CaCO_3$	+	HCl	→	$CaCl_2$	+ CO_2 + H_2O

3 Balance the equation.

- There are **more** chlorine atoms and hydrogen atoms on the products side than on the reactants side, so **balance** chlorine by doubling the amount of hydrochloric acid.
- The amount of chlorine and hydrogen on both sides is now equal. This gives you a **balanced equation**.

4 Write a balanced symbol equation using state symbols

$$CaCO_3(s) + 2HCl(aq) \longrightarrow CaCl_2(aq) + CO_2(g) + H_2O(l)$$

Carbon Compounds

Carbon is found in **group 4** of the periodic table. It has four electrons in its outer shell and so with four more electrons it has eight electrons in its outer shell.

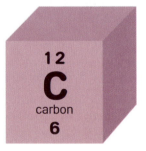

12
C
carbon
6

This means that carbon is able to form four covalent bonds with other atoms:

- Carbon atoms can bond together to make chains of (almost) unlimited size.
- Carbon atoms can bond with other atoms to form **carbon compounds**.

Organic compounds contain carbon and hydrogen and are the basis of life. They are found in all living things. The study of this is called **organic chemistry**.

Key Words

Alkane • Alkene • Covalent bond • Double bond • Saturated hydrocarbon • Unsaturated hydrocarbon

Alkanes

A **hydrocarbon** is an organic compound containing hydrogen and carbon only. The 'spine' of a hydrocarbon is made up of a chain of carbon atoms.

Alkanes are **saturated hydrocarbons**:

- They contain **single covalent** carbon–carbon bonds.
- Each carbon atom is bonded to four other atoms.

Methane, CH_4

$$H - \underset{\underset{H}{|}}{\overset{\overset{H}{|}}{C}} - H$$

Ethane, C_2H_6

$$H - \underset{\underset{H}{|}}{\overset{\overset{H}{|}}{C}} - \underset{\underset{H}{|}}{\overset{\overset{H}{|}}{C}} - H$$

Propane, C_3H_8

$$H - \underset{\underset{H}{|}}{\overset{\overset{H}{|}}{C}} - \underset{\underset{H}{|}}{\overset{\overset{H}{|}}{C}} - \underset{\underset{H}{|}}{\overset{\overset{H}{|}}{C}} - H$$

Butane, C_4H_{10}

$$H - \underset{\underset{H}{|}}{\overset{\overset{H}{|}}{C}} - \underset{\underset{H}{|}}{\overset{\overset{H}{|}}{C}} - \underset{\underset{H}{|}}{\overset{\overset{H}{|}}{C}} - \underset{\underset{H}{|}}{\overset{\overset{H}{|}}{C}} - H$$

Alkenes

Alkenes are **unsaturated hydrocarbons**. Alkenes…

- contain one **double** covalent carbon–carbon bond
- have some carbon atoms that are bonded to less than four other atoms.

Ethene, C_2H_4

Propene, C_3H_6

Testing for Alkanes and Alkenes

A simple test to distinguish between alkanes and alkenes is to add **bromine water**:

- Alkenes will **decolourise** bromine water as the alkene reacts with it.
- Alkanes have **no effect** on bromine water.

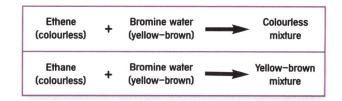

| Ethene (colourless) | + | Bromine water (yellow–brown) | → | Colourless mixture |
| Ethane (colourless) | + | Bromine water (yellow–brown) | → | Yellow–brown mixture |

(HT) Making Ethanol from Ethene

Ethene can be reacted with water at a high temperature in the presence of a catalyst to produce ethanol:

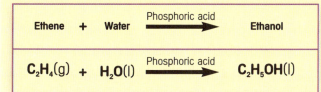

| Ethene | + | Water | Phosphoric acid → | Ethanol |
| C_2H_4(g) | + | H_2O(l) | Phosphoric acid → | C_2H_5OH(l) |

Ethanol is used…

- in the main part of the manufacture of industrial methylated spirits
- in greener fuels, e.g. Gasohol
- as a solvent in cosmetics and perfumes.

Synthesis

Cracking

Cracking involves the breaking down of long-chain hydrocarbon molecules into more useful short-chain hydrocarbon molecules.

When alkanes are cracked, alkanes and alkenes are formed:

In preparation for cracking to take place, the long-chain hydrocarbon is heated until it vaporises. The vapour is then passed over a heated catalyst where a **thermal decomposition** reaction takes place.

In the laboratory, cracking is carried out using this apparatus:

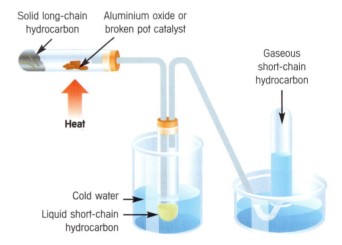

Monomers to Polymers

A **monomer** is a short-chain hydrocarbon molecule based on alkenes. **Unsaturated monomers** join together to form long-chain hydrocarbon molecules called **polymers**.

For example, when ethene molecules join together they form a polymer called poly(ethene) by a process called **addition** polymerisation.

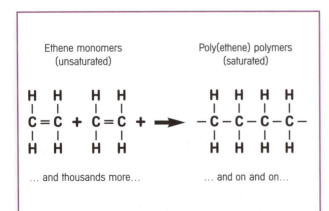

The general equation for addition polymerisation is shown here:

You will need to be able to draw the displayed **formula** of a polymer if you're given the displayed formula of a monomer (and vice versa), e.g. propene monomer to poly(propene) polymer:

Properties of Polymers

Polymers have properties that make them very useful.

In general, polymers…
- have good strength
- have good elasticity
- are corrosion resistant
- are good electrical and thermal insulators
- have low densities compared with metals that they are used to replace
- can be made any colour (by adding colour to the raw product)
- can be easily moulded into shape.

Types of Polymer

Polymers can be divided into two groups:
- **thermoplastics**
- **thermosetting**.

Thermoplastics can be **easily softened** by heating and remoulded into new shapes. This is because their polymer chains have **weak inter-molecular forces**, which can be easily overcome by applying heat. The heat softens the polymer and enables it to be remoulded as the chains slip easily over each other.

Thermosetting polymers can be softened and moulded into shape the first time they're heated but they **can't be re-softened or remoulded**. This is because the molecules are **cross linked**, which makes the polymer rigid and strong, and unable to be reshaped when reheated.

Thermoplastics

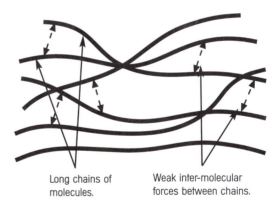

Long chains of molecules.

Weak inter-molecular forces between chains.

Thermosetting Polymers

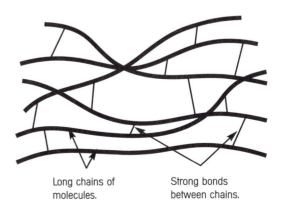

Long chains of molecules.

Strong bonds between chains.

Key Words

Addition • Cracking • Formula • Monomer • Polymer • Thermoplastic • Thermosetting • Unsaturated monomers

Synthesis

Changing Properties of Plastics

By adding chemical substances during the initial manufacturing process, you can make the properties of plastics desirable for their end uses.

Cross-linking agents are added to thermoplastics to encourage the molecules to form cross links. This gives the plastic stability.

Plasticisers are added to make thermoplastics **more flexible**. Plasticisers fill the gaps between the chains, allowing them to slip over each other more easily.

UV (ultraviolet) and thermal **stabilisers** (preservatives) are added to extend a plastic's life.

Disposing of Plastics

There are various ways of disposing of plastics but some of these methods can be harmful to the environment.

Burning plastics produces carbon dioxide, which contributes to the Greenhouse Effect. Some plastics shouldn't be burned as they produce toxic fumes, e.g. burning PVC produces hydrogen chloride gas.

Plastics are put in **landfill sites**. But, as most plastics are non-biodegradable, they will not decompose and rot away. This means that plastic waste builds up.

Crude Oil

This bar chart shows…
* the relative amounts of each fraction in crude oil
* the demand for each fraction in crude oil.

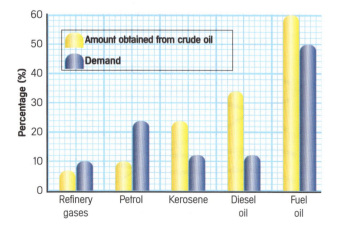

The demand for some fractions is **greater than** the supply, especially for shorter-chain hydrocarbons, e.g. petrol. This is because they release energy more easily when burned, so they make better fuels.

Longer-chain hydrocarbons are broken down into more useful shorter-chain hydrocarbons by cracking. The compounds that are produced have a variety of uses, e.g. to fuel transport, to heat homes and to make substances for drugs.

As crude oil runs out, supply decreases, but demand remains the same and so prices increase. Scientists are always trying to find new ways of making the substances that crude oil provides.

Vegetable Oils

Vegetable oils are used in cooking and are **unsaturated**.

They are liquids at room temperature because they have high levels of **monounsaturated** and **polyunsaturated fats**.

Monounsaturated fats have only **one double** carbon–carbon bond per molecule.

Polyunsaturated fats have **two or more double** carbon–carbon bonds per molecule.

An Example of One Unit in a Molecule of Monounsaturated Fat

$$CH_3(CH_2)_7CH = CH(CH_2)_7COOCH_2$$

Unit repeated many times

An Example of One Unit in a Molecule of Polyunsaturated Fat

$$CH_3(CH_2)_5CH = CHCH = CH(CH_2)_7COOCH_2$$

Unit repeated many times

Hydrogenated Vegetable Oil

Monounsaturated and polyunsaturated oils are less viscous than saturated oils. This is because they have double carbon–carbon bonds, meaning there are fewer bonds with hydrogen and therefore less inter-molecular hydrogen bonding.

Vegetable oil can be hardened by adding hydrogen, which breaks the double carbon–carbon bonds. Enough double bonds have to be **hydrogenated** to achieve the right viscosity.

Removing some or all of the double carbon–carbon bonds will raise the melting point of vegetable oil and can increase its shelf life, as the oil is less likely to go rancid.

An Example of One Unit in a Molecule of Monounsaturated Fat

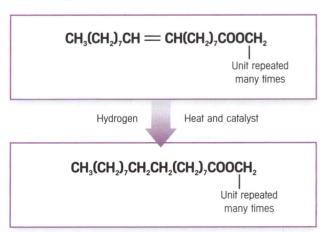

$$CH_3(CH_2)_7CH = CH(CH_2)_7COOCH_2$$

Unit repeated many times

Hydrogen   Heat and catalyst

$$CH_3(CH_2)_7CH_2CH_2(CH_2)_7COOCH_2$$

Unit repeated many times

Key Words

Fat • Hydrogenate • Monounsaturated • Polyunsaturated

Synthesis

Product Development

The outcomes of some new reactions can be predicted using **computer modelling** to compare the new substance to other known substances.

In any reaction between an acid and a base that you carry out, you can predict the product because you will always obtain a salt and water.

Developing a new drug is a lengthy and expensive process, so the drug industry is looking into ways in which timescales and costs can be reduced.

Using **computer simulation technology** means that more compounds can be developed because the computer programmes do all the initial work:

- Drug companies select the right target compounds as they compare new structures with known structures and get rid of those that have been found to be **toxic** in the past.
- Only the best compounds are **synthesised** in the laboratory to be tested on humans.
- The most effective compound is then tested on a larger group of volunteers.
- A final **toxicological study** is done on the compound before it goes into production.

HT You will need to be able to calculate the number of possible products from a staged synthesis experiment.

For example, the following **staged synthesis** shows the reaction of ammonia to produce nitric acid. In this staged synthesis there are four products, but only nitrogen monoxide, nitrogen dioxide and nitric acid are potentially useful.

Stage 1

Ammonia	+	Oxygen	$\longrightarrow$	Nitrogen monoxide	+	Water

$$4NH_2(g) + 5O_2(g) \longrightarrow 4NO(g) + 6H_2O(l)$$

Stage 2

Nitrogen monoxide	+	Oxygen	$\longrightarrow$	Nitrogen dioxide

$$2NO(g) + O_2(g) \longrightarrow 2NO_2(g)$$

Stage 3

Nitrogen dioxide	+	Oxygen	+	Water	$\longrightarrow$	Nitric acid

$$4NO_2(g) + O_2(g) + 2H_2O(l) \longrightarrow 4HNO_3(aq)$$

Relative Formula Mass

The **relative formula mass** of a compound is the relative atomic masses of all atoms present in its formula added together.

Example

Calculate the relative formula mass of water, H_2O.

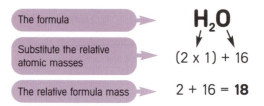

The formula	H_2O
Substitute the relative atomic masses	$(2 \times 1) + 16$
The relative formula mass	$2 + 16 = \mathbf{18}$

Key Words

Empirical • Sustainable development • Synthesis • Toxicity

Empirical Formula

Empirical **formula** is the simplest formula that represents the ratio of atoms in a compound.

Example

Find the empirical formula of an oxide of iron, produced by reacting 1.12g of iron with 0.48g of oxygen. (Relative atomic masses: Fe = 56; O = 16).

Identify the mass of the elements in the compound

Masses: Fe = 1.12, O = 0.48

Divide these masses by their relative atomic masses

No. of iron atoms $= \frac{1.12}{56} = 0.02$

No. of oxygen atoms $= \frac{0.48}{16} = 0.03$

Identify the ratio of atoms in the compound

Ratio = x 100 $\Big($ 0.02 : 0.03 $\Big)$ x 100

2 : 3

Empirical formula = **Fe_2O_3**

HT Calculating Mass

Calculate how much calcium oxide can be produced from 50kg of calcium carbonate. (Relative atomic masses: Ca = 40; C = 12; O = 16).

1. Write down the equation.
2. Work out the relative formula mass of each substance involved in the equation.
3. The question only mentions calcium oxide and calcium carbonate, so you can now ignore the carbon dioxide. You just need the ratio of mass of reactant to mass of product.
4. Use the ratio to calculate how much calcium oxide can be produced.

1
$CaCO_3 \rightarrow CaO + CO_2$

2
$40 + 12 + (3 \times 16) \rightarrow (40 + 16) + [12 + (2 \times 16)]$

3
100 : 56

4
If 100kg of $CaCO_3$ produces 56kg of CaO, then 1kg of $CaCO_3$ produces $\frac{56}{100}$ kg of CaO, and 50kg of $CaCO_3$ produces $\frac{56}{100} \times 50$
= **28kg of CaO**.

Atom Economy

Chemical reactions often produce more than one **product**, but not all of these products are 'useful'.

Atom economy is a measure of the amount of reactants that end up as useful products.

Scientists make sure that the process they use gives **high atom economy**.

Reactions with high atom economy are important for **sustainable development** as they prevent waste.

Synthesis

HT Calculating Atom Economy

The atom economy of any reaction can be calculated using this equation:

$$\text{Atom economy} = \frac{\text{Mass of (atoms in) useful product}}{\text{Total mass (of atoms) of product}} \times 100\%$$

Example

How economic is the production of zinc chloride when zinc carbonate is reacted with hydrochloric acid? (Relative atomic masses: Zn = 65; Cl = 35.5; H = 1; C = 12, O = 16)

First, write down the equation of the reaction:

Zinc carbonate	+	Hydrochloric acid	→	Zinc chloride	+	Water	+	Carbon dioxide

$$ZnCO_3(s) + 2HCl(aq) \rightarrow ZnCl_2(aq) + H_2O(l) + CO_2(g)$$

Mass of atoms in useful product, $ZnCl_2$:

Zn x 1 = 65 x 1 = 65
Cl x 2 = 35.5 x 2 = 71
= 136

Mass of atoms in waste product, H_2O:

H x 2 = 1 x 2 = 2
O x 1 = 16 x 1 = 16
= 18

Mass of atoms in waste product, CO_2:

C x 1 = 12 x 1 = 12
O x 2 = 16 x 2 = 32
= 44

$$\text{Atom economy} = \frac{136}{(136 + 18 + 44)} \times 100$$

$$= \frac{136}{198} \times 100 = \mathbf{68.69\%}$$

Calculating Yields

There are two yields in a reaction:

- **Theoretical yield** – calculated from the masses of atoms.
- **Actual yield** – the actual mass obtained from the reaction in the experiment.

From these two yields, you can calculate the **percentage yield**:

$$\text{Percentage yield} = \frac{\text{Actual yield}}{\text{Maximum theoretical yield}} \times 100\%$$

Example

264g of silver chloride was obtained from the reaction of magnesium chloride and silver nitrate. (Relative atomic masses: Ag = 108; Cl = 35.5)

First, write down the equation of the reaction:

Silver nitrate	+	Magnesium chloride	→	Silver chloride	+	Magnesium nitrate

$$2AgNO_3(aq) + MgCl_2(aq) \rightarrow 2AgCl(s) + Mg(NO_3)_2(aq)$$

Work out the formula mass for AgCl:

Ag x 1 = 108 x 1 = 108
Cl x 1 = 35.5 x 1 = 35.5
= 143.5

Theoretical yield for AgCl = 143.5 x 2 = 287g

2AgCl means there are two formulae of AgCl produced.

$$\text{Percentage yield} = \frac{\text{Actual yield}}{\text{Theoretical yield}} = \frac{264}{287} \times 100$$

$$= \mathbf{91.9\%}$$

Key Words

Percentage yield • Theoretical yield

Glossary of Key Words

Addition – when molecules react together to produce a larger molecule with no other product.

Alkane – a saturated hydrocarbon with the general formula C_nH_{2n+2}

Alkene – an unsaturated hydrocarbon (with only one double carbon–carbon bond) with the general formula C_nH_{2n}

Covalent bond – a bond between two atoms in which the atoms share a pair of electrons.

Cracking – a process used to break down long-chain molecules into (more useful) short-chain molecules.

Double bond – a covalent bond that involves the sharing of two pairs of electrons.

Empirical – the simplest ratio of atoms in a compound as represented by the chemical formula.

Fat – oily / greasy substance that breaks down into fatty acids and glycerol.

Formula – shows the relative numbers of the different kinds of atoms in a compound.

Hydrogenate – to add hydrogen to an unsaturated compound.

Monomer – a small molecule that chemically bonds to other monomers to produce a polymer.

Monounsaturated – an organic compound that only contains one double carbon–carbon bond per molecule.

Polymer – a long-chain molecule made up of a large number of monomers that have combined together during polymerisation.

Polyunsaturated – an organic compound with more than one double carbon–carbon bond per molecule.

Saturated hydrocarbon – a molecule that contains only hydrogen and carbon; it has no double covalent carbon–carbon bond so has the maximum possible number of hydrogen atoms.

Sustainable development – development that meets the needs of the present without compromising the ability of future generations to meet their own needs.

Synthesis – the formation of a compound from its constituent elements.

Thermoplastic – a plastic that will soften when heated and can be moulded into shape. The process of heating and remoulding can be repeated many times.

Thermosetting – a plastic that can be moulded only the first time it's heated. It can't be softened or remoulded when reheated but it will decompose in extreme heat.

Toxicity – a harmful effect of a chemical substance on a living organism with the severity of toxicity produced being directly proportional to the exposure concentration and time.

Unsaturated hydrocarbon – a molecule that contains only hydrogen and carbon; it has at least one double carbon–carbon bond so some of the carbon atoms are bonded to less than four other atoms.

Unsaturated monomers – small molecules that can join together to form polymers. They contain double or triple carbon bonds and can be saturated by adding hydrogen.

HT **Percentage yield** – the mass of product obtained expressed as a percentage of the calculated theoretical yield.

Theoretical yield – the maximum mass of product that can be produced as calculated using relative atomic masses.

Practice Questions

1 What do the following state symbols mean?

a) (aq) .... **b)** (s) ....

c) (g) .... **d)** (l) ....

2 What is a hydrocarbon?

....

3 What is the difference between an alkane and an alkene?

....

....

4 What happens when bromine water is added to an alkene?

....

5 Give three uses of ethanol.

a) ....

b) ....

c) ....

6 What type of chemical reaction is involved during the cracking of a long-chain hydrocarbon?

....

7 What is the difference between a thermoplastic and a thermosetting polymer?

....

....

8 Give three ways in which the properties of plastics can be changed.

a) ....

b) ....

c) ....

9 Circle the correct options in the following sentences.

Vegetable oils are used in **cooking** / **cleaning** and are **saturated** / **unsaturated**. They are **liquids** / **solids** at room **temperature** / **pressure** because they have **low** / **high** levels of monounsaturated and polyunsaturated **fats** / **oils**.

10 Why are double carbon–carbon bonds removed from vegetable oil?

....

....

11 What is the relative formula mass of $CaCO_3$ (relative atomic masses: Ca = 40, C = 12 and O = 16)? Tick the correct option.

A 100 ◯	B 51 ◯
C 300 ◯	D 124 ◯
E 85 ◯	F 150 ◯

12 Why are reactions with high atom economy important?

....

HT

13 How many useful products are there when ammonia is converted to nitric acid?

....

14 How much CaO can be produced from 25kg of $CaCO_3$ (relative atomic masses: Ca = 40, C = 12 and O = 16)? Tick the correct option.

A 28kg ◯	B 51 kg ◯
C 14kg ◯	D 56kg ◯
D 32kg ◯	E 6kg ◯

15 What is the theoretical yield and actual yield of a chemical reaction?

a) Theoretical yield ....

....

b) Actual yield ....

....

In Your Element

The Periodic Table and the Elements

All things are made of **elements**. The known elements are arranged in the **periodic table**.

The first modern periodic table by Mendeleev had gaps for elements that were yet to be discovered. Mendeleev was also able to predict the properties of one of these elements, silicon, before it was discovered.

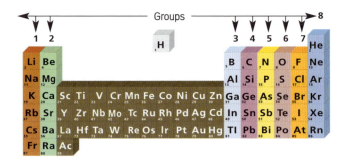

The Atom

Elements are made up of atoms. An atom has…

- a **nucleus** containing **protons** and **neutrons**
- **electrons** surrounding the nucleus, arranged in shells.

The table below shows the relative masses and charges of the different particles. An atom has the **same number** of protons as electrons, so the atom as a whole has **no electrical charge**.

Atomic Particle		Relative Mass	Relative Charge
Proton	●	1	+1
Neutron	●	1	0
Electron	✗	Negligible	-1

An Atom

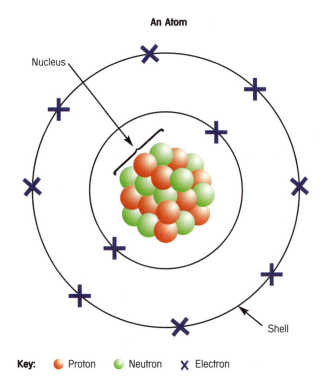

Key: ● Proton ● Neutron ✗ Electron

Atomic Number and Relative Atomic Mass

All elements in the periodic table have an atomic number and a relative atomic mass:

- The **atomic number** can be found at the bottom of the symbol. It is the number of protons in the atom.
- The **relative atomic mass** can be found at the top of the symbol and is the mass of a particular atom compared to a twelfth of the mass of a carbon atom.

Key Words

Atomic number • Electron • Isotopes • Mass number • Neutron • Nucleus • Periodic table • Proton • Relative atomic mass

Isotopes

All the atoms of a particular element have the same number of protons. This number is unique to each element and is its atomic number.

Isotopes are atoms of the same element that have different numbers of neutrons. Isotopes have the **same atomic number** but a **different mass number**. The mass number is the total number of protons and neutrons in the atom.

Isotopes of the same element have the same chemical properties because they have the same number of protons (and electrons).

For example, chlorine has two isotopes:

 Chlorine

$$^{35}_{17}\text{Cl}$$

17 protons
17 electrons
18 neutrons $(35 - 17)$

2 Chlorine

$$^{37}_{17}\text{Cl}$$

17 protons
17 electrons
20 neutrons $(37 - 17)$

HT Relative Atomic Mass

Relative atomic mass is a weighted average value for all the different isotopes of an element.

Chemists use relative atomic masses because they take into account the relative isotopic masses and the abundance of each one.

Example 1: Chlorine

Naturally occurring chlorine is made up of 75% of $^{35}_{17}\text{Cl}$ and 25% of $^{37}_{17}\text{Cl}$, i.e. in a ratio of 3:1.

So, for every four atoms of chlorine, three of them are $^{35}_{17}\text{Cl}$ and one of them is $^{37}_{17}\text{Cl}$.

This means that the total atomic mass of these four atoms =

$(3 \times 35) + (1 \times 37) = 142$

So, the relative atomic mass of chlorine can be calculated:

$$\frac{142}{4} = \textbf{35.5}$$

N.B. Relative atomic masses and relative isotopic masses are not always whole numbers but are often rounded up or down for ease of calculations.

Example 2: Magnesium

Magnesium is made up of 80% of $^{24}_{12}\text{Mg}$, 10% of $^{25}_{12}\text{Mg}$ and 10% of $^{26}_{12}\text{Mg}$, i.e. in the ratio of 8:1:1.

So, for every ten atoms of magnesium, eight of them are $^{24}_{12}\text{Mg}$, one of them is $^{25}_{12}\text{Mg}$ and one of them is $^{26}_{12}\text{Mg}$.

This means that the total atomic mass of these ten atoms =

$(8 \times 24) + (1 \times 25) + (1 \times 26) = 243$

So, the **relative atomic mass** of magnesium can be calculated:

$$\frac{243}{10} = \textbf{24.3}$$

In Your Element

Electronic Configuration

Electronic configuration tells you how the electrons are arranged around the nucleus of an atom in shells:

- The first shell can hold a maximum of two electrons.
- The shells after this can hold a maximum of eight electrons.

Electronic configuration is written as a series of numbers, for example aluminium is 2.8.3.

There is a connection between the number of outer electrons and the position of an element in a group:

- Elements in group 1 have one electron in their outer shell.
- Elements in group 2 have two electrons in their outer shell.

The electronic configurations of the first 20 elements are shown below:

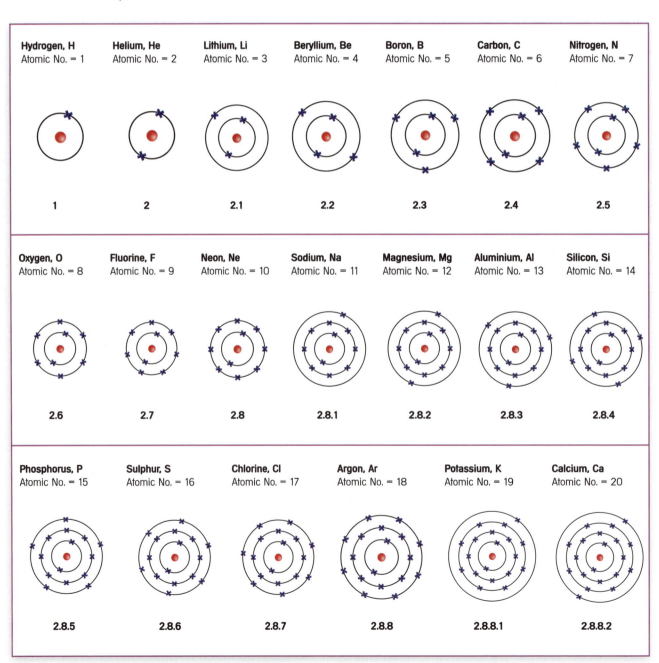

| Hydrogen, H Atomic No. = 1 | Helium, He Atomic No. = 2 | Lithium, Li Atomic No. = 3 | Beryllium, Be Atomic No. = 4 | Boron, B Atomic No. = 5 | Carbon, C Atomic No. = 6 | Nitrogen, N Atomic No. = 7 |
| 1 | 2 | 2.1 | 2.2 | 2.3 | 2.4 | 2.5 |

| Oxygen, O Atomic No. = 8 | Fluorine, F Atomic No. = 9 | Neon, Ne Atomic No. = 10 | Sodium, Na Atomic No. = 11 | Magnesium, Mg Atomic No. = 12 | Aluminium, Al Atomic No. = 13 | Silicon, Si Atomic No. = 14 |
| 2.6 | 2.7 | 2.8 | 2.8.1 | 2.8.2 | 2.8.3 | 2.8.4 |

| Phosphorus, P Atomic No. = 15 | Sulphur, S Atomic No. = 16 | Chlorine, Cl Atomic No. = 17 | Argon, Ar Atomic No. = 18 | Potassium, K Atomic No. = 19 | Calcium, Ca Atomic No. = 20 |
| 2.8.5 | 2.8.6 | 2.8.7 | 2.8.8 | 2.8.8.1 | 2.8.8.2 |

Reactivity of Elements

How an element reacts depends on…

- the number of electrons in the outer shell
- the distance the outer shell is from the nucleus.

Reactivity of Alkali Metals

The **alkali metals** (found in group 1) all have one electron in their outer shell.

They become **more reactive** as the atomic number increases because the outer electron becomes further away from the influence of the nucleus and so an electron is **more easily lost**.

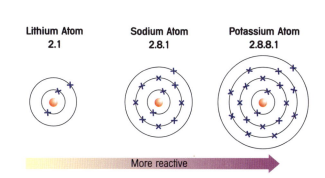

Lithium Atom
2.1

Sodium Atom
2.8.1

Potassium Atom
2.8.8.1

More reactive

Reactivity of the Halogens

The halogens (found in group 7) all have seven electrons in their outer shell.

They become **less reactive** as the atomic number increases because the outer electron becomes further away from the influence of the nucleus and so an extra electron is **less easily attracted**.

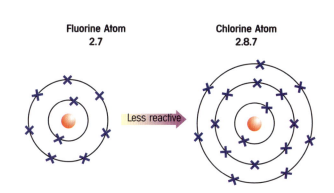

Fluorine Atom
2.7

Chlorine Atom
2.8.7

Less reactive

Reactivity of the Noble Gases

The noble gases (found in Group 0 / 8) all have eight electrons in the outer shell (except for helium, which has two).

This means electrons are arranged in such a way as to discourage any bonding with other elements.

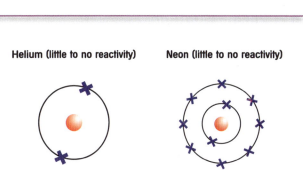

Helium (little to no reactivity)

Neon (little to no reactivity)

Key Words

Electronic configuration

In Your Element

Ionic Bonding

An **ionic bond** occurs between a **metal** and a **non-metal** atom.

It involves a transfer of electrons from one atom to another.

Ionic bonding results from the formation of electrically charged **ions**. Each ion has eight electrons in the outer shell (like the noble gas atoms), which can be…

- positively charged (**cations**)
- negatively charged (**anions**).

Example 1

Sodium (Na) and chlorine (Cl) bond ionically to form sodium chloride, NaCl.

1. The sodium atom has 1 electron in its outer shell.
2. The electron is transferred to the chlorine atom.
3. Both atoms now have 8 electrons in their outer shell.
4. The atoms become ions, Na^+ and Cl^-.
5. The compound formed is sodium chloride, NaCl.

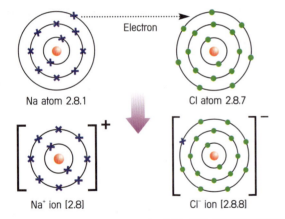

Na atom 2.8.1   Electron   Cl atom 2.8.7

Na^+ ion [2.8] Cl^- ion [2.8.8]

Example 2

Magnesium (Mg) and oxygen (O) bond ionically to form magnesium oxide, MgO.

1. The magnesium atom has 2 electrons in its outer shell.
2. These 2 electrons are transferred to the oxygen atom.
3. Both atoms now have 8 electrons in their outer shell.
4. The atoms become ions, Mg^{2+} and O^{2-}.
5. The compound formed is magnesium oxide, MgO.

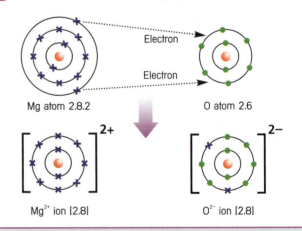

Mg atom 2.8.2   Electron   Electron   O atom 2.6

Mg^{2+} ion [2.8] O^{2-} ion [2.8]

Predicting Formulae

Ionic compounds are **neutral** because the charges on the ions cancel each other out. If you know the charge on the ions, you can predict the **formula** for any ionic compound.

For example, magnesium ions have a 2+ charge, Mg^{2+} and chloride ions have a 1- charge, Cl^-.

The charge on two chloride ions balances out the charge on one magnesium ion: $Mg^{2+} + 2 \times Cl^-$ = $MgCl_2$.

Key Words

Binary salt • Conductivity • Electrode • Electrolysis • Formulae • Ion • Ionic bonding

Ionic Structures

Ionic compounds, e.g. sodium chloride (NaCl) are made up of a giant lattice, held together by the forces of attraction between the positive ions and the negative ions.

Sodium chloride is an example of a **binary salt** as it's made up of anions and cations.

Ionic compounds...
- have high melting and boiling points due to the strong electrostatic forces of attraction
- **conduct** electricity when molten or in solution because the charged ions are free to move about
- are crystalline due to the regular arrangement of their ions.

Electrolysis

Electrolysis is the breaking down of a compound containing ions into its elements using a direct current.

When a direct current is passed through a liquid containing ions, the ions move to the **electrode** of opposite charge:
- Positively charged ions move towards the **negative cathode**.
- Negatively charged ions move towards the **positive anode**.

When the ions reach the electrodes, they lose their charges:
- Positive ions gain electrons from the cathode.
- Negative ions lose electrons to the anode.

When this happens, atoms of elements are formed. For example, when copper is needed in a pure form, it's purified by electrolysis.

HT The reactions at the electrodes can be written as **half equations**. This means that you write separate equations for what is happening at each of the electrodes during electrolysis.

During the purification of copper using copper(II) sulphate solution, the following half equations tell us what is happening at each electrode.

At the positive anode, the copper atoms lose electrons and go into solution as ions:

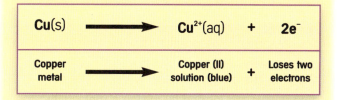

$$Cu(s) \longrightarrow Cu^{2+}(aq) + 2e^-$$

| Copper metal | | Copper (II) solution (blue) | + | Loses two electrons |

At the negative anode, positively charged ions gain electrons to become atoms:

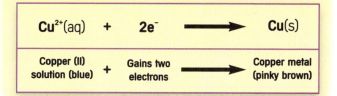

$$Cu^{2+}(aq) + 2e^- \longrightarrow Cu(s)$$

| Copper (II) solution (blue) | + | Gains two electrons | | Copper metal (pinky brown) |

Positive electrode

Negative electrode

Chlorine gas released

Copper deposited

Copper chloride solution

In Your Element

Electrolysis of Aluminium Oxide

Molten aluminium oxide is a molten binary salt. It can be electrolysed to produce aluminium. The equation for this process is as follows:

Aluminium oxide	$\longrightarrow$	Aluminium	+	Oxygen
$2Al_2O_3(l)$	$\longrightarrow$	$4Al(l)$	+	$3O_2(g)$

HT At the anode:

$$2O^{2-}(g) \xrightarrow{\text{Oxidation}} O_2(g) + 4e^-$$

At the cathode:

$$Al^{3+}(l) + 3e^- \xrightarrow{\text{Reduction}} Al(l)$$

Pure Metals

Pure metals only contain atoms of that element. Most of those metals extracted from the ground need to be purified.

Pure metals have the following properties:
- They make good conductors of heat and electricity.
- They are strong and hard.
- They are dense.
- They are **malleable**.
- They are solids at room temperature (except mercury).
- They produce sonorous sound when struck.
- They are shiny when polished.
- They have high melting points.

Key Words

Alloy • Malleability

Alloys

Many metals are more useful when they're not pure. **Alloys** are formed by mixing a metal with other metals. This can change the properties of the metal. The resulting alloy has a **greater range of uses** than the main metal.

An alloy can have…
- a lower melting point
- increased corrosion resistance
- increased chemical resistance
- increased strength and hardness.

Pure iron is soft and it bends and corrodes easily:
- Carbon is present in iron to produce mild steel, which is hard and strong.
- Nickel and chromium are added to iron to produce stainless steel, which is hard and rustproof.

Pure aluminium has many uses but it isn't as strong as steel:
- Copper is added to aluminium to make it stronger.
- Zinc is added to aluminium to make it stronger and improve its corrosion resistance.

Glossary of Key Words

Alloy – a metal made by mixing a metal with another metal; the alloy has different properties from the pure metal.

Atomic number – (of an element) the number of protons in the nucleus of an atom; it is also the number of electrons orbiting the nucleus in an atom.

Binary salt – a simple salt that's made of a cation and an anion.

Conductivity – the ability of a substance to conduct electrical current (and heat).

Electrode – the charged rod or plate that carries electricity in and out of a molten or aqueous solution of salt during electrolysis.

Electrolysis – the splitting up of a molten or aqueous solution of salt by passing a direct electrical current through a liquid containing ions.

Electronic configuration – the arrangement of electrons around the nucleus of an element. It can be represented by diagrams or numbers and always starts with the inner shell.

Electron – a particle that carries a negative charge; arranged in shells (or energy levels) around the nucleus of an atom.

Formulae – shows the relative numbers of atoms of different elements in a compound.

Ion – a positively or negatively charged particle formed when an atom (or group of atoms) loses or gains electrons.

Ionic bonding – charged ions that are held together by forces of attraction.

Isotopes – atoms of the same element that contain different numbers of neutrons.

Malleability – the ability of a metal to be hammered into different shapes without cracking or breaking.

Mass number – the total number of protons and neutrons in the nucleus of an atom.

Neutron – an atomic particle found in the nucleus of an atom; it has a relative mass of 1 but it doesn't have a charge.

Nucleus – the central part of an atom made up of small particles called protons and neutrons (except hydrogen).

Periodic table – a list of all the different kinds of elements, arranged in order of increasing atomic number, in a pattern according to the electronic configuration and the way in which they behave.

Proton – an atomic particle found in the nucleus of an atom; it has a relative mass of 1 and it has a positive charge.

Relative atomic mass – the average mass of an atom of an element compared with a twelfth of the mass of a carbon atom.

Practice Questions

1. Which of the following is the correct mass number and atomic number for sulphur-32? Tick the correct option.

   A Mass number = 16, Atomic number = 32. ⬚

   B Mass number = 15, Atomic number = 32. ⬚

   C Mass number = 32, Atomic number = 16. ⬚

   D Mass number = 16, Atomic number = 16. ⬚

2. Which of the following correctly describes the difference between isotopes of an element? Tick the correct option.

   A More nuclei ⬚

   B Different number of neutrons per atom ⬚

   C Different number of protons per atom ⬚

   D Less nuclei ⬚

HT

3. How is the relative atomic mass of an element calculated?

   ....

4. Fill in the missing words to complete the following sentences.

   How an elements reacts depends on the number of .... in the outer shell and the

   distance the outer shell is from the ....

5. How many electrons are in the outer shells of atoms of elements in the following groups?

   a) Group 1

   ....

   b) Group 3

   ....

   c) Group 5

   ....

6 Circle the correct options in the following sentences.

a) Atoms lose or gain **electrons** / **protons** in order to have eight in their **outer** / **inner** shell.

b) To form an ion, **electrons** / **protons** are either accepted or donated by other **elements** / **atoms**.

7 What is the formula of the ionic compound lithium oxide?

8 What is the difference between cations and anions?

9 What is a binary salt?

HT

10 During the electrolysis of aluminium oxide, what happens at the anode? Write the half equation.

11 An alloy is made from a mixture of metals. What kind of properties can alloys have? Tick the correct option(s).

A A higher melting point than the pure metal

B A lower melting point than the pure metal

C Strong under tension and compression

D Increased strength and hardness

E Increased chemical resistance

F Ability to be hammered into shape without cracking

Chemical Structures

Covalent Bonds

Covalent bonds occur when **electrons are shared** between non-metal atoms. Covalent bonds can occur between atoms of the same element or atoms of different elements. Covalent bonds result in the formation of **molecules**.

A **single covalent bond** is formed when two atoms share **one pair** of electrons, e.g. chlorine atoms join together to form diatomic chlorine molecules, Cl_2 (as with all **halogens**):

- The atoms both gain one electron to have eight outer shell electrons.
- They share one pair of electrons in a single covalent bond.

A **double bond** is formed when **two pairs** of electrons are shared, e.g. oxygen atoms join together to form diatomic oxygen molecules, O_2:

- The atoms both gain two electrons to have eight outer shell electrons.
- They share two pairs of electrons in a double bond.

A **triple bond** is formed when **three pairs** of electrons are shared, e.g. nitrogen atoms join together to form diatomic nitrogen molecules, N_2:

- The atoms both gain three electrons to have eight outer shell electrons.
- They share three pairs of electrons in a triple bond.

A Single Covalent Bond

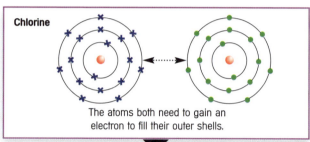

Chlorine

The atoms both need to gain an electron to fill their outer shells.

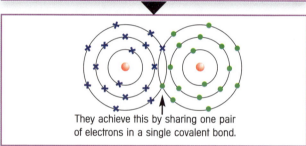

They achieve this by sharing one pair of electrons in a single covalent bond.

HT Examples of Covalent Compounds

You need to be able to draw dot and cross diagrams for the following simple molecules:

Molecule	Water H_2O	Carbon dioxide CO_2	Hydrogen H_2	Hydrogen chloride HCl
Method 1	H O H	O C O	H H	H Cl
Method 2	H–O–H	O = C = O	H – H	H – Cl

60

Chemical Structures

Simple Molecules

Simple molecular covalent structures have relatively few atoms in their molecules.

There are **strong** forces **between the atoms** in the molecules but there are **weak inter-molecular forces**.

This means that simple molecular covalent structures…

* have low melting and boiling points
* can't **conduct** electricity
* are often gases at room temperature.

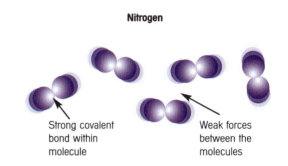

Nitrogen

Strong covalent bond within molecule

Weak forces between the molecules

Key Words

Conductivity • Covalent bond • Halogen • Inter-molecular force • Simple molecular covalent structure

HT The Halogens

The **halogens** are found in group 7 of the periodic table. The most common halogens are…

* chlorine
* bromine
* iodine.

The halogens are **diatomic molecules**. They can be solid, liquid or gas at room temperature depending on the strength of the forces holding the molecules together.

The attraction between **chlorine molecules** is weak so the melting and boiling points are low. Chlorine is a gas at room temperature.

The attraction between **bromine molecules** is slightly stronger than chlorine but the attraction is still weak. Bromine's melting and boiling points are still low but it's a liquid at room temperature.

The attraction between **iodine molecules** is stronger still. The molecules don't come apart from each other easily and, therefore, iodine is a solid at room temperature.

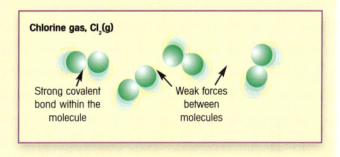

Chlorine gas, $Cl_2(g)$

Strong covalent bond within the molecule

Weak forces between molecules

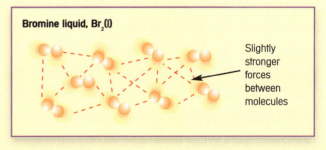

Bromine liquid, $Br_2(l)$

Slightly stronger forces between molecules

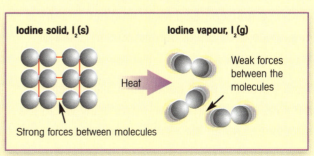

Iodine solid, $I_2(s)$

Iodine vapour, $I_2(g)$

Heat

Weak forces between the molecules

Strong forces between molecules

Chemical Structures

Giant Molecules

Giant molecular covalent structures have many atoms joined to each other in their molecules. This makes their properties very different from those of simple molecular substances.

Each carbon atom in the structures of diamond and graphite shares its electrons with the atoms next to it so that they all have eight electrons in their outer shells.

Diamond (a form of carbon) is a giant covalent structure where each carbon atom forms **four covalent bonds** with other carbon atoms. Diamond…

- has very high melting and boiling points
- is very hard
- is unable to conduct electricity.

Graphite (a form of carbon) is a giant covalent structure where each carbon atom forms **three covalent bonds** with other carbon atoms in a **layered structure**. The layers can slide past each other. Graphite…

- has very high melting and boiling points
- is soft and slippery
- is able to conduct heat and electricity as a result of delocalised electrons within each molecule
- has weak forces of attraction between layers.

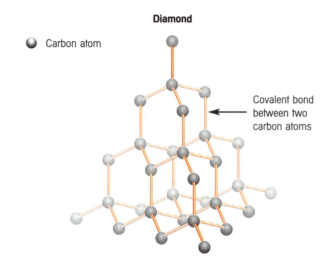

Diamond

Carbon atom

Covalent bond between two carbon atoms

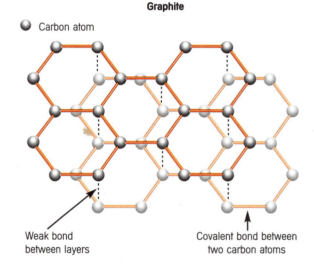

Graphite

Carbon atom

Weak bond between layers

Covalent bond between two carbon atoms

Bonding in Metals

Metal atoms form **giant crystalline structures**.

The atoms are packed tightly together so the outer electrons get separated from the atom. The result is a lattice structure of positive ions in a **sea of free electrons.**

Metals are **very good conductors** of electricity because their electrons can move freely within the structure, carrying the electric charge.

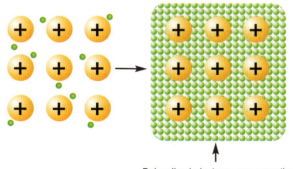

Metal Atoms in a Crystalline Structure

Delocalised electrons can carry the electric charge or thermal (heat) energy

Chemical Structures

Buckminsterfullerenes

A third form of carbon was discovered in 1985. Scientists fired lasers at graphite to see what would happen and, by chance, different forms of carbon were found. The most stable and common form was **carbon-60**.

Carbon-60 became known as **Buckminsterfullerene**. Fullerenes are closed carbon cages found in common soot. The carbon-60 was isolated and synthesised and its structure was examined.

The following properties were found:

- It was a closed carbon structure with unsaturated carbon–carbon bonding; both double and single.
- It behaved unusually and showed stronger stability than diamond.

- It could bounce and return to its original shape.
- It could spin at high speeds.
- It wasn't very reactive but it was the only form of carbon that could be dissolved.
- It was 1 nanometre in diameter (1nm); this was an early milestone in nanotechnology research.

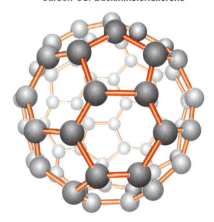

Carbon-60: Buckminsterfullerene

Carbon Nanotubes

The **carbon nanotube** was developed in 1991 from half a molecule of Buckminsterfullerene. It looks like a one layer of graphite that has been made into a tube. It was found to be the strongest form of carbon.

Carbon nanotubes (CNTs) are flexible and are able to bend up or down to contact an electrode.

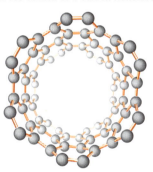

Cross-section of a Carbon Nanotube

Uses of Carbon Structures

There are many uses for carbon fullerenes and nanotubes, for example…

- superconductors for use in conducting electricity because they have no electrical resistance
- transistors and diodes (in circuits)
- ion storage for batteries
- reinforcement in buildings, because they are very flexible
- industrial catalysts.

Key Words

Buckminsterfullerene • Carbon nanotube • Diamond • Giant molecular covalent structure • Graphite

Chemical Structures

Representing Molecular Structures

All molecules have a structure.

The structure can be…
- simple, e.g. water
- complex, e.g. diamond

Molecular structures can be represented in…
- two dimensions (2-D)
- three dimensions (3-D).

Structure of Sodium Chloride

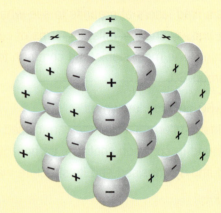

2-D Models

Drawing 2-D models is good for representing small molecules and atoms.

But, it's difficult to see…
- how atoms are arranged within the structure of the molecule
- how electrons are arranged around the nucleus of an atom (to help explain chemical reactions).

Fluorine atom

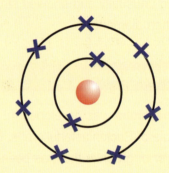

3-D Models

3-D models can be…
- 'stick and ball models'
- computer simulations.

Using computer simulation means that the models can be moved and viewed from different angles.

They can show how adding individual atoms to the structure can change the shape of the molecule.

They can also show how the electrons are arranged and how they move around the nucleus of an atom.

Computer simulations enable us to study the geometry and properties of molecules.

Methane

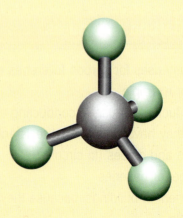

Chemical Structures

Chemical-based Therapy

Chemical-based therapy refers to any form of medication that is taken to relieve symptoms of an illness or ailment.

Chemical-based therapy can be…
- prescribed medicines
- **homeopathic** treatments.

HT Effectiveness of Treatment

Chemotherapy is a drug treatment that's widely used in the treatment of cancer. It's used to try to kill cancer cells and stop them from spreading.

Chemotherapy is very effective but it causes **unpleasant side effects**, e.g. hair loss, sickness and tiredness. Patients that have this treatment are monitored for many years because the illness can sometimes return.

Antibiotics are drugs used to destroy bacteria that cause infections and illnesses, e.g. tuberculosis, cholera and tetanus. They have been used successfully for years.

Antibiotics can cause side effects and they can interfere with the effectiveness of other medications. If antibiotics are overused, the bacteria can become resistant to them, so they should only be taken when necessary.

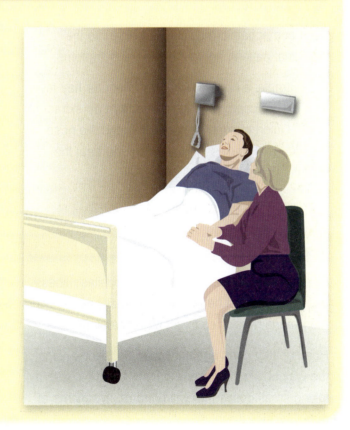

How Medicines Work

Most medicines are designed to…
- replace substances that are deficient or missing in the body
- alter the activity of the cells
- destroy infectious microorganisms and destroy abnormal cells.

Key Words

Homeopathic

Chemical Structures

Homeopathic Treatments

Homeopathic treatments can alter the activity of cells. They use very weak, diluted doses of compounds or drugs that, if strong enough, would cause symptoms of the illness in a healthy person.

The word homeopathy comes from Greek words meaning 'similar suffering'.

Homeopathic medicine works in the following way:

1 Tiny doses of drugs (which would cause symptoms of an illness) are put in the person.
2 This causes the body to kickstart the natural healing process.

Each homeopathic medicine is tailored to the individual patient; not to the general symptoms.

For example, a homeopathic treatment for hay fever uses *allium cepa*, which is made from an extract of onion. Onion makes the eyes sting and the nose run, etc. This makes the body begin to treat the symptoms naturally.

Arguments Against Homeopathy

Scientific theory uses the way of 'opposites': illness and disease must be fought off naturally or by taking man-made medicines to get rid of the symptoms.

Homeopathy goes **against scientific theory**, using the way of 'similars': treating illness and disease by taking small doses that will bring on symptoms of that illness or disease.

Studies and research have been carried out into the effectiveness of homeopathic treatments, but no conclusive evidence has been taken.

Some scientists believe that homeopathic treatments have a **placebo effect**. This means that people believe they experience a therapeutic and healing effect from an inert medicine or ineffective therapy.

Glossary of Key Words

Buckminsterfullerenes – a form of carbon that has molecules made of 60 carbon atoms. The atoms fold around and join together to make a ball shape. The carbon atoms form shapes of pentagons and hexagons like a football.

Carbon nanotube – a form of carbon made from a single layer of graphite (a graphene), rolled up to make a tube.

Conductivity – a substance's ability to conduct thermal and electric energy.

Covalent bond – a bond between two atoms in which both atoms share a pair of electrons.

Diamond – a substance made of carbon that has a giant molecular structure. Each carbon atom is held to the four carbon atoms around it by very strong covalent bonds.

Giant molecular covalent structure – a molecule in which all of the atoms are linked together by a network of bonds extending throughout the crystal, e.g. diamond, graphite.

Graphite – a substance made of carbon that has a giant molecular structure. Each carbon atom is bonded to three other carbon atoms by strong covalent bonds, forming a sheet of carbon atoms. Many of these sheets are layered together and held in place by weak forces of attraction. Each layer of graphite is a single giant molecule.

Halogen – non-metals found in Group 7 of the periodic table. They exist as diatomic molecules.

Homeopathic – a holistic medicine used to treat the whole state (mind and body); based on the principle of treating like with like. It uses extreme dilutions of animal, vegetable or mineral preparations to stimulate the human body's healing system.

Inter-molecular force – found in simple molecular substances such as water, it is the weak force of attraction that holds the molecules together. These forces can easily be overcome by heating the substance.

Simple molecular covalent structure – atoms in the molecules are held together with strong covalent bonds; the molecules are held together within their structure by weak inter-molecular bonds. They have low melting and boiling points.

Practice Questions

1 Circle the correct options in the following sentences.

   a) A covalent bond occurs between **metal** / **non-metal** atoms and forms very **strong** / **weak** bonds in which electrons are **transferred** / **shared**.

   b) A covalent bond can occur between **elements** / **atoms** of the same element or atoms of different elements and forms **molecules** / **compounds**.

2 How many electrons are shared in a triple bond?

3 Why are chlorine and oxygen described as diatomic molecules?

4 Which two forces make some covalent structures simple molecules?

   a)

   b)

HT

5 Why is iodine a solid at room temperature with a relatively high boiling point compared with other halogens?

6 Which form of carbon has four covalent bonds formed by each atom?

7 Which of the following are properties of graphite? Tick the correct options.

   A Very low melting point ☐

   B Poor conductor of heat ☐

   C Slippery ☐

   D Good conductor of electricity ☐

   E Hard ☐

   F High boiling point ☐

8 How do metals conduct electricity?

....

9 For what uses have scientists proposed carbon fullerenes and nanotubes? Tick the correct option(s).

    A Ion storage for batteries ⬭

    B Superconductors ⬭

    C Electrical resistors ⬭

    D Reinforcement in buildings ⬭

    E Artificial gem stones ⬭

10 How many carbon atoms are there in the Buckminsterfullerene molecule? Tick the correct option.

    A 40 ⬭   **B** 50 ⬭

    C 60 ⬭   **D** 100 ⬭

HT

11 List two disadvantages of representing molecules as 2-D models.

    a) ....

    b) ....

12 Circle the correct options in the following sentence.

Antibiotics are drugs used to **destroy** / **grow** bacteria that cause **infections** / **diseases** and illness, e.g. **tuberculosis** / **influenza**.

13 State three things that most medicines are designed to do.

    a) ....

    b) ....

    c) ....

14 What does the term *placebo effect* mean?

....

How Fast? How Furious?

Rates of Reaction

Three factors that affect the **rate of reaction** are…

- the **temperature** of the reaction
- the **surface area** of the solid reactant
- the **concentration** of the reactants.

The results of many rates of reaction experiments can be recorded accurately using data-logging equipment.

HT Chemical reactions usually occur when particles collide with each other with sufficient energy. This is called the **collision theory**. Increasing the frequency and energy of collisions increases the rate of the reaction.

Low Temperature	High Temperature
Slower reaction rate as there are fewer successful collisions. This is because particles… • move slowly • collide less often and with less energy. 	Faster reaction rate as there are more successful collisions. This is because particles… • move quickly • collide more often and with greater energy. 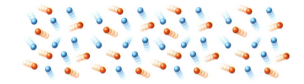
Small Surface Area	**Large Surface Area**
Slower reaction rate as there are fewer successful collisions. This is because particles… • have a small surface area in relation to their volume • are less exposed to collisions so collide less often. 	Faster reaction rate as there are more successful collisions. This is because particles… • have a large surface area in relation to their volume • are more exposed to collisions so collide more often. 
Low Concentration	**High Concentration**
Slower reaction rate as there are fewer successful collisions. This is because particles… • are fewer in number per unit volume and are spread out • collide less often. 	Faster reaction rate as there are more successful collisions. This is because particles… • are greater in number per unti volume and are packed close together • collide more often. 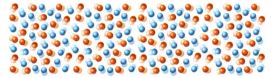

Changing Rates of Reactions

Calcium carbonate reacts with hydrochloric acid to produce calcium chloride.

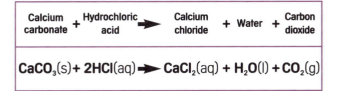

| Calcium carbonate | + | Hydrochloric acid | → | Calcium chloride | + | Water | + | Carbon dioxide |

$$CaCO_3(s) + 2HCl(aq) \longrightarrow CaCl_2(aq) + H_2O(l) + CO_2(g)$$

You can measure how long it takes for a given mass of calcium carbonate to react completely and plot your results on a graph.

Graph 1 shows that you can increase the rate of reaction by increasing the temperature of the solution.

The rate of reaction can also be found by measuring the amount of carbon dioxide given off every minute from a given amount of calcium carbonate.

Graph 2 shows that you can increase the rate of reaction by making the solid have a larger surface area, i.e. by crushing the calcium carbonate.

N.B. There's the same mass of calcium carbonate in both reactions, so the same volume of carbon dioxide is produced. It just takes different amounts of time.

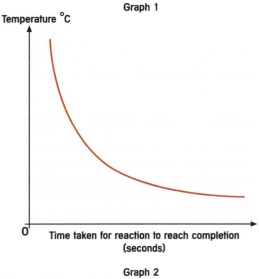

Graph 1

Temperature $^{\circ}C$

Time taken for reaction to reach completion (seconds)

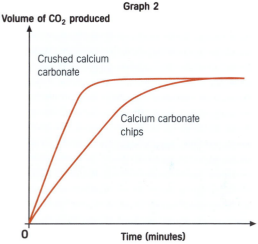

Graph 2

Volume of CO_2 produced

Crushed calcium carbonate

Calcium carbonate chips

Time (minutes)

Catalysts

Catalysts increase the rate of a chemical reaction, without being used up in the process. This means that only small amounts of them are needed.

Catalysts work by reducing the **activation energy** needed for a reaction to happen. This means that more collisions will be successful and the reaction will be faster.

They can provide a surface for the molecules to attach to, so they increase the chance of molecules bumping into each other.

Catalysts are used in industrial processes to speed up reactions and make production more economical.

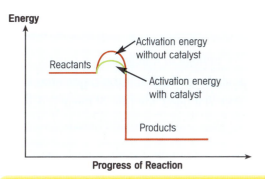

Energy

Activation energy without catalyst

Reactants

Activation energy with catalyst

Products

Progress of Reaction

Key Words

Catalyst • Concentration • Collision theory • Rate of reaction • Surface area • Temperature

How Fast? How Furious?

The following reaction shows the decomposition of hydrogen peroxide.

Hydrogen peroxide ⟶	Water	+ Oxygen
$2H_2O_2(aq)$ ⟶	$2H_2O(l)$	+ $O_2(g)$

You can measure the rate of this reaction by measuring the amount of oxygen given off at one-minute intervals.

A catalyst of manganese (IV) oxide can be added to increase the rate of reaction. With the catalyst, you can see plenty of fizzing as the oxygen is given off.

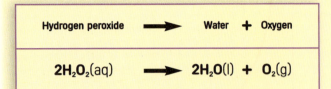

N.B. There's the same amount of hydrogen peroxide in both reactions, so the same volume of oxygen is produced at the end of the reaction. It just takes different amounts of time.

Without a catalyst

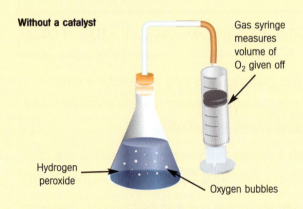

Gas syringe measures volume of O_2 given off

Hydrogen peroxide

Oxygen bubbles

With a catalyst

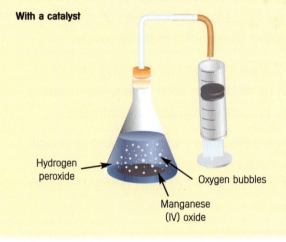

Hydrogen peroxide

Oxygen bubbles

Manganese (IV) oxide

Enzymes

Enzymes are **biological catalysts** that control the rate of chemical reactions in living organisms. If enzymes were not used, the rate of these reactions would be so slow that life wouldn't exist.

Enzymes work best under certain conditions of temperature and pH. Different enzymes work best at different optimum temperatures.

An enzyme can be **denatured** by extreme temperature and pH. This means that its shape is changed irreversibly and it can no longer affect the rate of reaction.

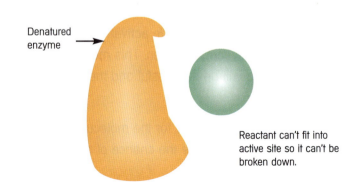

Denatured enzyme

Reactant can't fit into active site so it can't be broken down.

Temperature Changes in Reactions

All chemical reactions are accompanied by a **temperature change**.

Exothermic reactions are accompanied by a rise in temperature in their surroundings. They **give heat energy out** to their surroundings.

Examples of exothermic reactions include…
- combustion
- respiration in body cells
- hydrolysation of ethene to form ethanol
- neutralising alkalis with acids.

Endothermic reactions are accompanied by a fall in temperature in their surroundings. They **take heat energy in** from their surroundings.

Examples of endothermic reactions include…
- dissolving ammonium nitrate crystals in water
- the reaction between citric acid and sodium hydrogen carbonate solution
- polymerisation of ethene to poly(ethene)
- reduction of silver ions to silver in photography
- photosynthesis.

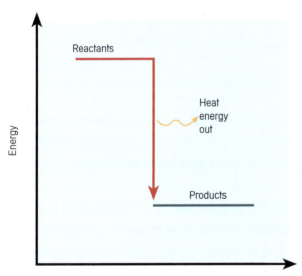

Exothermic Reaction

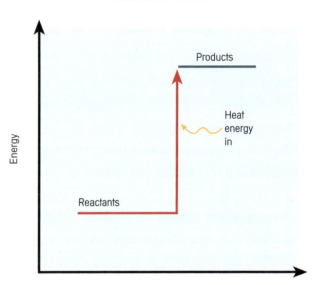

Endothermic Reaction

Making and Breaking Bonds

In a chemical reaction, the bonds in the reactants must be broken and new bonds made to form the products.

Chemical reactions that require **more energy to break bonds** than is released when bonds are formed are **endothermic** reactions.

Chemical reactions that release **more energy** when bonds are formed than is needed to break them are **exothermic** reactions.

Key Words

Endothermic reaction • Enzyme • Exothermic reaction

How Fast? How Furious?

Reversible Reactions

All chemical reactions are **reversible**. This means that the **products** can react together to produce the original **reactants**. For example, the decomposition of ammonium chloride is a reversible reaction:

- Solid ammonium chloride decomposes when heated to produce ammonia and hydrogen chloride gas.
- Ammonia reacts with hydrogen chloride gas to produce white ammonium chloride powder.

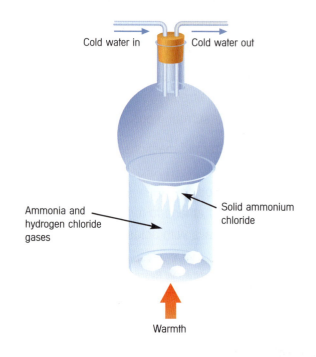

Cold water in   Cold water out

Ammonia and hydrogen chloride gases

Solid ammonium chloride

Warmth

Ammonium chloride	⇌	Ammonia	+	Hydrogen chloride
$NH_4Cl(s)$	⇌	$NH_3(g)$	+	$HCl(g)$

Reactions in Equilibrium

A reversible reaction will reach a state of **equilibrium** in a closed system (where no reactants are added and no products are removed).

This means that the reactions occur at exactly the same rate in both directions. A reaction that's in equilibrium will **never go to completion**.

HT It's possible to **change the position** of dynamic equilibrium in a reversible reaction, as the equilibrium will shift to try to cancel out any change that is introduced to the reaction.

When the **concentration** of the reactants in a reversible reaction is increased, this happens:

1. The rate of the forward reaction increases.
2. The rate of the reverse reaction also increases.
3. The rates of both reactions eventually even out, so equilibrium is restored.
4. The concentration at equilibrium of the products increases.

$$A + B \rightleftharpoons C + D$$

When the **temperature** of the reactants in a reversible reaction is increased, this happens:

1. The endothermic reaction will be favoured as more heat is taken in by the reverse reaction.
2. The rate of this reaction speeds up until the forward reaction begins to give out more heat.
3. Eventually both reactions even out, restoring equilibrium.

$$A + B \rightleftharpoons C + D + \text{Heat}$$

Increasing the pressure will favour the forward reaction as there are less molecules so it will reduce the volume of reactants, and therefore, reduce pressure and restore equilibrium.

$$A(g) + B(g) \rightleftharpoons C(g)$$

The Haber Process

Ammonia is neutralised by nitric acid in the production of **ammonium nitrate fertiliser**.

Ammonia, NH_3, can be made on a large scale in the Haber process. This process uses…

- nitrogen
- hydrogen.

Nitrogen and hydrogen gases combine in a **reversible reaction**: the nitrogen and hydrogen combine with each other at the same time as the ammonia decomposes. This makes it very difficult for the nitrogen and hydrogen to stay combined.

If the reaction takes place in a closed system, it will reach a stage of dynamic equilibrium. This means that there's a constant interchange between the **reactants** and **products**.

Nitrogen	+	Hydrogen	⇌	Ammonia
$N_2(g)$	+	$3H_2(g)$	⇌	$2NH_3(g)$

The following conditions are used:

- Temperature of 450°C.
- **Pressure** of 200 atmospheres.
- Iron catalyst.

HT It's important to get the maximum yield in the shortest time possible (see also page 76):

- At high temperature the yield is low as the ammonia decomposes as quickly as it's made, but at low temperature the reaction is slow.
- At high pressure the reaction is too expensive and the ammonia decomposes as quickly as it's made so less yield is obtained.
- A catalyst reduces the activation energy so that a good yield can be obtained from the temperature and pressure at a fast rate.

Key Words

Dynamic equilibrium • Equilibrium • Fertiliser • Haber process • Pressure • Reversible

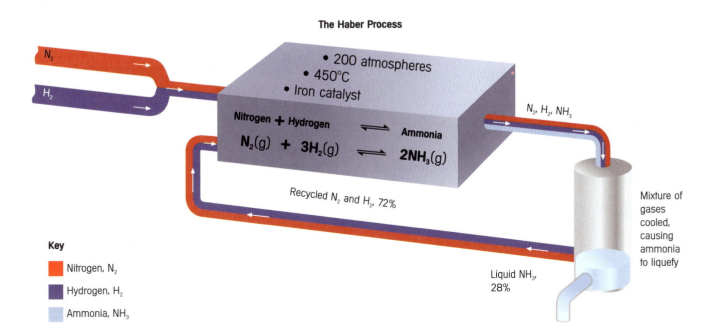

The Haber Process

- 200 atmospheres
- 450°C
- Iron catalyst

Nitrogen + Hydrogen ⇌ Ammonia

$N_2(g)$ + $3H_2(g)$ ⇌ $2NH_3(g)$

N_2, H_2, NH_3

Recycled N_2 and H_2, 72%

Mixture of gases cooled, causing ammonia to liquefy

Liquid NH_3, 28%

Key

- Nitrogen, N_2
- Hydrogen, H_2
- Ammonia, NH_3

How Fast? How Furious?

Fertilisers

Artificial Fertiliser	Organic Fertiliser
Advantages • They are easier to store, distribute and handle than **organic** alternatives. • They are produced to match crop requirements. • They help increase crop yield providing efficiently produced food that costs less. **Disadvantages** • They can be harmful if they get into drinking water. • They contain nitrates that can leak into lakes and rivers, causing eutrophication. • They can be expensive.	**Advantages** • They use and recycle natural waste. • They are not as dependent on fossil fuels, making them more sustainable than artificial fertilisers. • They encourage good soil structure and management. **Disadvantages** • More fertiliser is needed due to low nitrogen content. • They vary in efficiency. • They need to be converted to an inorganic form before they can be used. • They are messy to handle.

HT Balancing Ionic Compounds

Atoms have **no overall charge** because the negatively charged electrons balance the positively charged protons. When an atom…

- loses electrons it forms a positively charged ion
- gains electrons it forms a negatively charged ion.

Ionic compounds don't have an overall charge because the charges of the elements cancel each other out. You can work out the formulae for ionic compounds by balancing the number of electrons.

Example

Work out the ionic equation for ammonium sulphate.

Ion for ammonium = NH_4^+

An ammonium compound molecule that has lost 1 electron

Ion for sulphate = SO_4^{2-}

A sulphate compound molecule that has gained 2 electrons

Ammonium ion	+	Sulphate ion	→	Ammonium sulphate

$$NH_4^+(aq) \ + \ SO_4^{2-}(aq) \ \longrightarrow \ (NH_4SO_4)(aq)$$

The lowest common multiple of 1 and 2 is 2. So multiply the ammonium ion by 2, and the sulphate ion by 1:

$NH_4^+ \times 2 = 2^+ = \textbf{2NH}_4^+\textbf{(aq)}$ 2 ammonium ions

$SO_4^{2-} \times 1 = 2^- = \textbf{SO}_4^{2-}\textbf{(aq)}$ 1 sulphate ion

This gives the ratio of ammonia ions to sulphate ions, 2:1

Ammonia	+	Sulphuric acid	→	Ammonium sulphate

$$2NH_4^+(aq) \ + \ SO_4^{2-}(aq) \ \longrightarrow \ (NH_4)_2SO_4(aq)$$

Key Words

Organic

Glossary of Key Words

Catalyst – a substance that's used to speed up a chemical reaction without being used up in the process.

Concentration – a measure of the amount of a substance that is present within a specified volume of its solution; the more substance there is, the more concentrated the solution.

Dynamic equilibrium – the state in a reversible reaction when reactants are changing to products and the products are changing to reactants to maintain stable concentrations. There is a constant interchange between reactants and products.

Endothermic reaction – a chemical reaction that takes in energy from the surroundings in the form of heat.

Enzyme – a large protein molecule that is a biological catalyst. It helps reactions to take place at the low temperatures found in living organisms.

Equilibrium – the state in a reversible reaction when the amount of each substance stays the same and there appears to be no change.

Exothermic reaction – a chemical reaction that gives out energy to the surroundings in the form of heat.

Fertiliser – a substance that's used to supplement the mineral nutrients present in soil or replace those lost through crop removal.

Haber process – the name given to the industrial process of making ammonia from nitrogen and hydrogen.

Organic substances – substances that contain carbon and hydrogen.

Pressure – the measure of the forces exerted due to the collision of particles of gas within the walls of the container.

Rate of reaction – the rate at which reactants change to products.

Reversible – a chemical reaction that goes both forwards and backwards: reactants react to produce products and the products react to produce reactants.

Surface area – a measure of how much surface of a solid has been exposed. Generally, the smaller the particle then the greater the overall surface area in relation to its volume.

Temperature – the potential for heat transfer or the degree of hotness of an object.

HT Collision theory – theory that, in order for a reaction to take place, the particles must collide with each other and those collisions must have enough energy to be successful.

Practice Questions

1 What are three ways in which a rate of reaction can be increased?

   a) ....

   b) ....

   c) ....

2 Which of the following sentences can be used to describe a reactant with high concentration? Tick the correct option(s).

   A The particles are packed close together. ◯

   B More particles are exposed and available for collisions. ◯

   C There are more particles present in the same volume. ◯

   D The particles move with a greater energy. ◯

   E There are less particles present in the same volume. ◯

HT

3 How do chemical reactions usually occur?

   ....

   ....

4 What happens to the collision of particles when the rate of reaction is increased?

   ....

5 Fill in the missing word to complete the following sentence.

   Catalysts work by reducing the .... energy needed for a reaction to take place.

6 What is an enzyme?

   ....

7 Draw lines between the boxes to match each type of reaction to its correct description.

Exothermic		Requires more energy to break bonds than is released when new bonds are formed.
Endothermic		More energy is released when new bonds are formed than is needed to break bonds.

8 Circle the correct options in the following sentences.

a) Some chemical reactions are **irreversible** / **reversible**. This means that the **reactants** / **products** will react to give the reactants that we started with.

b) Chemical reactions are accompanied by a temperature change. Reactions that have a(n) **increase** / **decrease** in temperature are exothermic reactions and reactions that have a(n) **increase** / **decrease** in temperature are endothermic reactions.

9 What happens in a reaction that is at equilibrium?

10 What are the conditions that are chosen for the Haber Process?

a)

b)

c)

11 What happens to a reversible reaction in a closed system?

12 a) Give two advantages of using artificial fertilisers over natural fertilisers.

i)

ii)

b) Give two advantages of using natural fertilisers over artificial fertilisers.

i)

ii)

HT

13 a) What happens to an atom when it loses electrons?

b) What happens to an atom when it gains electrons?

As Fast As You Can!

Speed

Speed tells you how fast an object is moving. It's measured in metres per second (m/s), kilometres per hour (km/h) or miles per hour (mph).

For example...

- a cyclist who travels a distance of 8 metres every second has a **constant** speed of 8 metres per second (8m/s)

- a car travelling at a constant speed of 60 miles per hour (60mph) would travel a distance of 60 miles every hour.

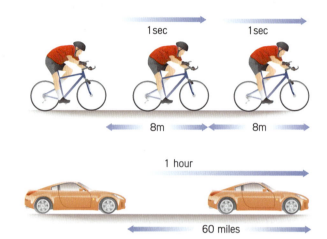

Velocity

Velocity describes the **speed** of an object in a stated **direction**. A quantity, such as velocity, that has both **magnitude** (size) and direction is known as a **vector** quantity.

The car in the diagram is travelling at a constant speed of 40km/h, but its velocity changes because its direction of movement changes, i.e. from east to south.

The direction of velocity is usually indicated by a positive (+) or a negative (-) sign. For example, if one car is travelling at +40km/h and another is travelling at -40km/h, they are simply travelling in opposite directions.

Displacement is another vector quantity. It's used to describe the distance covered in a certain direction.

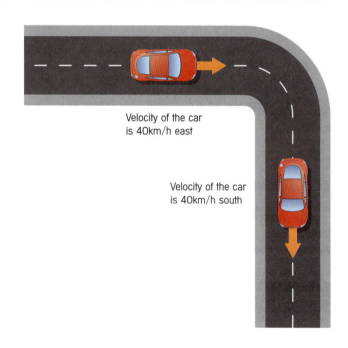

Velocity of the car is 40km/h east

Velocity of the car is 40km/h south

Calculating Velocity

You can calculate the velocity of an object using the following equation:

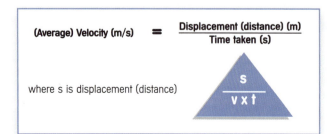

$$\text{(Average) Velocity (m/s)} = \frac{\text{Displacement (distance) (m)}}{\text{Time taken (s)}}$$

where s is displacement (distance)

$$\frac{s}{v \times t}$$

Example

An object moves a distance of 15m uniformly from rest in 5s, before returning to its starting position in 3s.

a) Calculate the velocity of the outward journey.

$$\text{Velocity} = \frac{\text{Displacement}}{\text{Time taken}} = \frac{15}{5} = \textbf{3m/s}$$

b) Calculate the velocity of the return journey.

$$\text{Velocity} = \frac{\text{Displacement}}{\text{Time taken}} = \frac{-15}{3} = \textbf{-5m/s}$$

Acceleration

The **acceleration** of an object is the rate at which its velocity changes; it's a measure of how quickly an object is **speeding up** or **slowing down**.

The change can be in magnitude and / or direction. So, acceleration is a vector quantity.

Acceleration is measured in metres per second per second (m/s^2). The cyclist in the diagram below increases his velocity by 2m/s every second. So, we can say that the acceleration of the cyclist is $2m/s^2$ (2 metres per second per second).

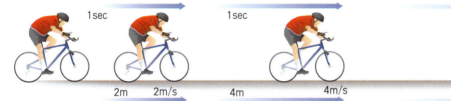

1sec	1sec	1sec
2m 2m/s	4m 4m/s	6m 6m/s

Calculating Acceleration

To work out the acceleration of any moving object you need to know two things:

• the **change in velocity**
• the **time taken** for the change in velocity.

You can then calculate the acceleration of the object using the following equation:

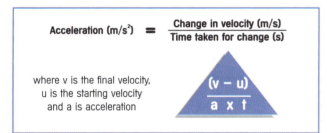

$$\text{Acceleration (m/s}^2) = \frac{\text{Change in velocity (m/s)}}{\text{Time taken for change (s)}}$$

where v is the final velocity, u is the starting velocity and a is acceleration

$$\frac{(v - u)}{a \times t}$$

When dealing with acceleration, remember the following two points:

• When velocity is increased by the **same amount** every second, the distance travelled each second **increases**.
• Deceleration is a negative acceleration, i.e. it describes an object that's slowing down.

Example

A cyclist accelerates uniformly from rest and reaches a velocity of 10m/s after 5s, before decelerating uniformly and coming to rest in a further 10s.

a) Calculate his acceleration for the first part of the journey.

$$\text{Acceleration} = \frac{\text{Change in velocity}}{\text{Time taken}} = \frac{10 - 0}{5}$$

$$= \textbf{2m/s}^2$$

b) Calculate his deceleration for the second part of the journey.

$$\text{Deceleration} = \frac{\text{Change in velocity}}{\text{Time taken}} = \frac{0 - 10}{10}$$

$$= \textbf{-1m/s}^2$$

N.B. Change in velocity = final velocity – starting velocity

Key Words

Acceleration • Displacement • Magnitude • Speed • Vector • Velocity

As Fast As You Can!

Velocity–Time Graphs

On a **velocity–time graph**…

- the slope represents the **acceleration** of an object – the steeper the **gradient**, the greater the acceleration
- the area underneath the line represents the total distance travelled (**displacement**).

Graph 1 shows an object that…

- has a constant velocity (100m/s), i.e. it isn't accelerating
- has travelled 500m.

Graph 2 shows an object that…

- is constantly accelerating by 20m/s^2
- has travelled 250m.

Graph 3 shows an object that…

- is constantly accelerating more rapidly, at 30m/s^2
- has travelled 375m.

Graph 4 shows an object that…

- is constantly decelerating by 30m/s^2, in other words constantly accelerating by −30m/s^2 (i.e. the object is slowing down)
- has travelled 375m.

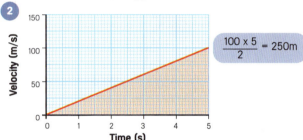

$100 \times 5 = 500m$

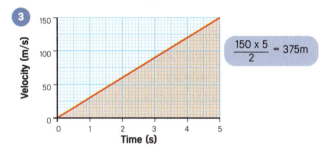

$\dfrac{100 \times 5}{2} = 250m$

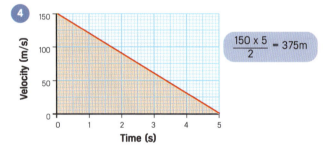

$\dfrac{150 \times 5}{2} = 375m$

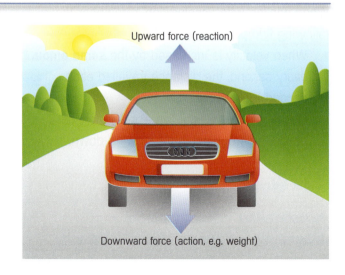

$\dfrac{150 \times 5}{2} = 375m$

Forces

Forces are pushes or pulls, e.g. friction, weight and air resistance. Forces may vary in size, and act in different directions. Force is measured in **Newtons** (N).

In general, the force exerted by an object (A) on another object (B) is known as an **action** force.

The force that object B exerts on object A is known as the **reaction** force. The reaction force will be equal in size but in the opposite direction to the action force. So, for every action, there's an equal and opposite reaction.

Upward force (reaction)

Downward force (action, e.g. weight)

Free-Body Force Diagrams

A **free-body force diagram** shows the forces acting on an object:

- Each force is shown by an arrow.
- The direction of the arrow indicates the direction of the force and the length of the arrow indicates the size of the force.

On the free-body force diagram, the arrows are all the same length, which means the forces are all equal, so the car is travelling at a constant speed.

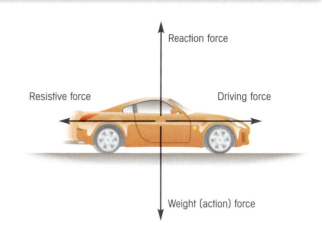

Forces and Movement

The movement of an object depends on all the forces acting upon it. The balance of these forces is called the **resultant force**.

A stationary car has two forces acting on it – the **weight** and reaction force. These two forces are equal, so the resultant force is zero and the car remains at rest.

A moving car has forces acting on it which affect its movement. For example, a car exerts a **driving force** and air resistance and friction are **resistive forces**. The balance of these two types of forces dictates the motion of the car:

You can calculate the resultant force using the following formula:

> **Resultant force (N) = Driving force (N) — Resistive forces (N)**

Example

A car has a driving force of 3000N. It's resisted by air resistance of 150N and friction from the tyres of 850N. Calculate the resultant force acting on the car.

Resultant force = Driving force − Resistive forces
= 3000N − (150N + 850N)
= **2000N**

1 When the driving force is greater than the resistive force (i.e. the resultant force is not zero), an unbalanced force will act on the car causing it to **accelerate**.	Driving force Resistive forces
2 When the resistive force is greater than the driving force (i.e. the resultant force is not zero), an unbalanced force will act on the car, causing it to **decelerate** (slow down).	Driving force Resistive forces
3 When the driving force is equal to the resistive force (i.e. the resultant force is zero), the forces acting on the car will be balanced, so the car will move at a **constant speed**.	Driving force Resistive forces

Key Words

Action • Gradient • Reaction • Resistance • Resultant force • Weight

As Fast As You Can!

Force, Mass and Acceleration

If an **unbalanced force** acts on an object (i.e. the resultant force is not zero) then the **acceleration** of the object will depend on…

- the **size** of the unbalanced force – the bigger the force, the greater the acceleration
- the **mass** of the object – the bigger the mass, the smaller the acceleration.

The following are examples of unbalanced forces:

1. If a boy pushes a trolley, he will exert an unbalanced force on it, which will cause it to move and accelerate.
2. If the boy pushes a trolley that has a bigger mass, it will move with a smaller acceleration than the first trolley.
3. If two boys push the same trolley, they will exert a larger force on it, so it will accelerate more quickly.

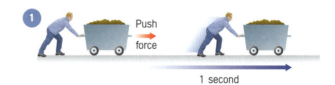

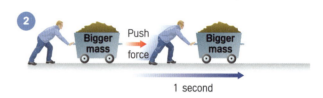

Calculating Force

You can calculate force using the following formula:

$$\text{Force (N)} = \text{Mass (kg)} \times \text{Acceleration (m/s}^2)$$

N.B. A Newton (N) is the force needed to give a mass of one kilogram an acceleration of one metre per second squared (1m/s².)

Example

A toy car of mass 800g accelerates with a force of 0.4N. Calculate its acceleration.

$$\text{Acceleration} = \frac{\text{Force}}{\text{Mass}}$$

$$= \frac{0.4\text{N}}{0.8\text{kg}} \quad \longleftarrow \text{Mass must be in kilograms}$$

$$= \textbf{0.5m/s}^2$$

What If...?

Spreadsheet 1 shows an example of a 'what if...?' situation. It calculates the acceleration of a car of mass 1 tonne for various driving forces.

Both the car mass and resistive forces can be altered and the acceleration re-calculated.

Spreadsheet 2 shows the results for the question 'what if m (car mass) is changed?'.

1

	A	B	C	D	E
	Driving Forces (N)	Resistive Forces (N)	Mass of car, m (tonnes)	Resultant Forces (N)	Acceleration, a (m/s²)
	500	300	1	200	0.2
	750	300	1	450	0.45
	1000	300	1	700	0.7

2

	A	B	C	D	E
	Driving Forces (N)	Resistive Forces (N)	Mass of car, m (tonnes)	Resultant Forces (N)	Acceleration, a (m/s²)
	500	300	1.2	200	0.17
	750	300	1.2	450	0.38
	1000	300	1.2	700	0.58

HT Momentum

Momentum is a measure of the state of movement of an object. It is affected by two factors:

- the **mass** of the object
- the **velocity** of the object (m/s).

Momentum is a **vector** quantity. You can calculate the momentum of an object using the following formula:

> Momentum (kg m/s) = Mass (kg) **X** Velocity (m/s)

Examples

1 A railway train with a mass of 40 tonnes is travelling with a uniform velocity of 15m/s. Calculate the train's momentum.

Momentum = Mass x Velocity

= (40 x 1000)kg x 15m/s

= **600 000kg m/s** 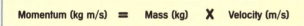 Convert tonnes into kg

2 A car of mass 1000kg is travelling at 10m/s. It then accelerates until it's travelling at 20m/s.

a) **i)** Calculate the car's initial momentum.

Momentum = Mass x Velocity

= 1000 x 10 = **10 000kg m/s**

ii) Calculate the car's final momentum.

Momentum = Mass x Velocity

= 1000 x 20 = **20 000kg m/s**

b) The car is loaded with an additional mass of 250kg.

i) Calculate the car's initial momentum.

Momentum = Mass x Velocity

= 1250 x 10 = **12 500kg m/s**

ii) Calculate the car's final momentum.

Momentum = Mass x Velocity

= 1250 x 20 = **25 000kg m/s**

As Fast As You Can!

Safety Features

Cars have lots of safety features to try to minimise injury and reduce the number of deaths that occur as a result of **collisions**. Most of them work by reducing the **momentum** over a longer period of time, which reduces the force experienced. For example…

- **crumple zones** within the car's structure help to absorb the momentum, meaning the force exerted on the people inside the car will be reduced, which results in fewer injuries
- **airbags** provide cushioning during impact
- **seatbelts** lock when the car brakes, exerting a force to counteract the momentum of the people wearing them.

Wearing a seatbelt whilst travelling in a motor vehicle greatly reduces the chance of death in the event of an accident:

- In 1992, it became compulsory for all front passengers to wear seatbelts and this led to a massive decline in the number of accident fatalities.
- In 1994, it became compulsory for all rear passengers to wear a seatbelt. This resulted in another significant reduction in the number of fatalities.

Key Words

Collision • Momentum • Stopping distance

HT Reducing Momentum

In the event of a collision, such as in a car accident, all of the momentum (and energy) of the impact is absorbed by the moving object and any passengers that may be inside it.

If the momentum can be reduced before impact, then the forces during impact can also be reduced:

- Crumple zones, air bags and seat belts reduce the change in momentum in a car collision.
- Padded cushion seats reduce the forces felt in a theme park ride.
- Cardboard egg holders absorb most handling forces to keep eggs intact.

Crumple zone

Stopping Distance

You can calculate the **stopping distance** of a vehicle using this formula:

$$\text{Stopping distance} = \text{Thinking distance} + \text{Braking distance}$$

- **Thinking distance** is the distance travelled by the vehicle from the point when the driver realises they need to apply the brakes to when they actually apply them.
- **Braking distance** is the distance travelled by the vehicle from the point when the driver applies the brakes to when the vehicle actually stops.

Factors Affecting Stopping Distance

Stopping distance is affected by the following:
- the driver's reaction time
- the mass of the vehicle
- the conditions of the vehicle and the road
- the speed of the vehicle.

The **driver's reaction time** (i.e. the time it takes from the point the driver realises they need to apply the brakes to when they actually apply them) affects the thinking distance only. It has no effect on the braking distance.

The following would increase the driver's reaction time:
- drinking alcohol or taking drugs
- being tired or distracted.

The **mass of a vehicle** affects the braking distance only. It has no effect on the thinking distance. If the mass of the vehicle is increased, i.e. by passengers, baggage, etc., it has greater momentum, which increases the braking distance.

The **condition of the vehicle and the road** may also affect the stopping distance. For example, the car may have worn tyres, or the road may be wet, icy or uneven. All these conditions will reduce the friction between the tyres and the road and increase the braking distance.

The **speed of the vehicle** affects both the thinking distance and the braking distance. The chart below shows how the thinking distance and braking distance of a vehicle under normal driving conditions depend on the speed of the vehicle.

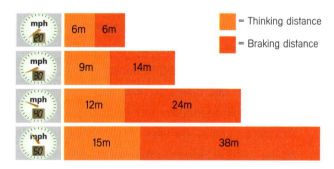

Risk Assessment

Risk is a perceived measure of the probability of something happening. It can't be calculated with any degree of certainty.

Probability can take any value between 0 and 1 and is usually expressed as a fraction, decimal or a percentage.

Risks can be…
- **imposed** (e.g. coal mining, operating machinery) **or**
- **voluntary** (smoking, rock climbing, etc.).

People's perception of risk may differ widely due to their degree of familiarity with that risk, and a person's willingness to take part in a risky activity may also depend upon the rewards offered, e.g. the adrenaline rush experienced.

As Fast As You Can!

Forces Acting on Falling Objects

Falling objects experience two forces…

- the downward force of **weight**, W (↓) which always stays the same
- the upward force of **air resistance**, R, or drag (↑)

Terminal Velocity

1 When a skydiver jumps out of an aeroplane they initially accelerate due to the force of gravity.

2 As they fall, they experience the frictional force of air resistance (R) in the opposite direction. But, this is not as great as W so they continue to accelerate.

HT

3 As their **speed** increases, so does the air resistance acting on them.

4 Eventually, R is equal to W. This means that the resultant force acting on them is now zero and their falling speed becomes constant. This speed is called the **terminal velocity**.

5 When they open their parachute, unbalanced forces act again because the upward force of R is now greatly increased and is bigger than W.

6 This causes their speed to decrease and as their speed decreases so does R.

7 Eventually R decreases until it is equal to W. The forces acting are once again balanced and for the second time they fall at a steady speed, slower than before though, i.e. at a new terminal velocity.

Key Words

Terminal velocity

Glossary of Key Words

Acceleration – the rate at which a body changes its velocity.

Action – a push or pull force that acts on an object.

Collision – an impact between two or more objects.

Displacement – the distance covered in a certain direction (a vector).

Gradient – a measure of how steep a line or slope is; can be positive or negative.

Magnitude – a measure of size.

Momentum – a measure of the state of motion of an object; given by mass x velocity; measured in kg m/s

Reaction – the force that is equal in size but opposite in direction to an action.

Resistance – a force that opposes motion.

Resultant force – the total force acting on an object (all the forces combined).

Speed – the rate at which a body moves.

Stopping distance – how long it takes a vehicle to stop; the sum of the thinking distance and the braking distance.

Vector – a quantity that has both magnitude (size) and direction.

Velocity – the speed at which an object moves in a particular direction.

Weight – the vertical force of an object; the product of mass and gravitational field strength; measured in Newtons (N).

HT **Terminal velocity** – the constant velocity reached by a falling body (i.e. when gravitational force is equal to the frictional forces acting on a body).

Practice Questions

1 Choose the correct words from the options given to complete the following sentences.

direction	magnitude	speed	velocity	vector	scalar	location

a) The .... of an object is the .... with which it is travelling

in a stated ....

b) This type of quantity has both direction and .... and is known as a

.... quantity.

2 A rocket launched from the ground reaches a height of 36 000m in 3 minutes before returning to Earth.

a) Calculate the velocity of the rocket on its outward journey. (Make sure you convert the minutes into seconds before carrying out your calculation.)

....

....

b) What is the rocket's overall displacement?

....

3 Fill in the missing words to complete the following sentence.

a) The acceleration of an object is the .... at which its ....

changes.

b) This is a .... quantity and has units of ....

4 The velocity–time graph shows the motion of a cyclist starting a race.

a) Calculate the cyclist's acceleration.

....

....

b) Why is the acceleration constant?

....

5 This car is travelling at a steady speed along a horizontal road.

a) Draw a free-body force diagram to show the forces acting on the car.

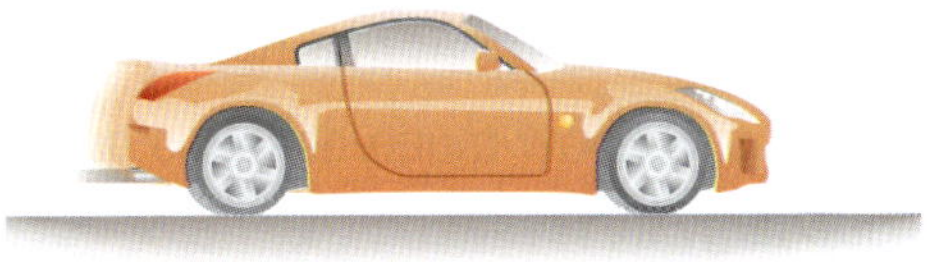

b) What happens to the car if the air resistance is greater than the driving force?

HT

6 An aeroplane of mass 100 000kg is moving along the runway with a uniform velocity of 12m/s. Calculate the momentum of the aeroplane.

7 Which of the following features reduce the momentum and force of impact in car collisions? Tick the correct options.

A Airbags ⬡   **B** Air brakes ⬡   **C** Seatbelts ⬡   **D** Crumple zones ⬡

8 Which of the following conditions affect the stopping distance of a vehicle? Tick the correct options.

A The condition of the vehicle ⬡   **B** The mass of the vehicle ⬡

C The momentum of the vehicle ⬡   **D** The driver's reaction time ⬡

9 The diagram shows the forces acting on a skydiver during his descent.

a) What do the following letters represent?

i) R ....   **ii)** W ....

HT **b)** Describe what happens when R and W are equal.

Roller Coasters and Relativity

Potential Energy

An object with **mass** (kg) lifted above the ground gains **potential energy** (PE), which is also known as **gravitational potential energy** (GPE). The additional height gives it the potential to do work when it falls, e.g. a diver on a diving board has gravitational potential energy.

Potential energy (J)	=	Mass (kg)	X	Acceleration of free-fall (N/kg)	X	Change in height (h)
PE = m x g x h						

Acceleration of free-fall is also referred to as **gravitational field strength** (g), which is a constant and has a value of ~10N/kg. This means that every 1kg of matter near the surface of the Earth experiences a downwards force of 10N due to gravity.

Example
A skier of mass 80kg gets on a ski lift that takes him from a height of 100m to a height of 300m above ground. By how much does his gravitational potential energy increase?

GPE = m x g x h
    = 80kg x 10N/kg x (300m − 100m)
    = 80kg x 10N/kg x 200m = **160 000J**

N.B. When a diver jumps off a diving board, or when a skier sets off down a slope, there's a transfer of energy from gravitational potential energy to kinetic energy.

Kinetic Energy

Kinetic energy is the energy an object has because of its movement. If it's moving, it has kinetic energy, e.g. a moving car or lorry has kinetic energy.

Kinetic energy (J)	=	$\frac{1}{2}$	X	Mass (kg)	X	Velocity^2 (m/s)^2
KE = $\frac{1}{2}$ x m x v^2						

Example
A lorry of mass 2050kg is moving at a **constant speed** of 6m/s. How much kinetic energy does it have?

Kinetic energy = $\frac{1}{2}$ x Mass x **Velocity**^{2}
         = $\frac{1}{2}$ x 2050kg x (6m/s)^2
         = $\frac{1}{2}$ x 2050 x 36
         = **36 900J**

Electrical Energy

The amount of **electrical energy** in an electric motor or other appliance is given by the relationship:

Electrical energy (J)	=	Voltage (V)	X	Current (A)	X	Time (s)
E = V x I x t						
Where I is current						

*N.B. **Voltage** is also known as **potential difference**.*

Example
A circuit is powered by a 1.5V cell that provides a **current** of 0.6A. Calculate how much energy is used by the circuit if it's switched on for 30 seconds.

Electrical energy = Voltage x Current x Time
          = 1.5V x 0.6A x 30s
          = **27J**

Roller Coasters and Relativity

Conservation of Energy

The principle of the **conservation of energy** says that energy can't be made or lost, only changed from one form into another.

The principle of conservation of energy can be seen in **roller coasters**. A roller coaster's energy is constantly changing between **gravitational potential energy** and **kinetic energy**, and the straight and curved sections of track serve to heighten the **acceleration**, **speed** and **forces** experienced.

The initial height gained by the roller coaster dictates the size and shape of the remainder of the ride. The other hills or loops in the ride will always be lower than the height of the initial one.

The more gravitational potential energy that is built up in the initial lift, the more kinetic energy is produced for the rest of the ride, and the faster the speed of the ride.

1 On most roller coasters the cars start high up with a lot of GPE or they're lifted mechanically, building up GPE.

2 After it reaches its highest point, the roller coaster starts to move down the first hill and the GPE is gradually being transferred into kinetic energy. Gravity, together with the mass of the cars and the passengers, applies a constant downward force which makes the cars accelerate down the hill. The roller coaster track simply serves to channel this force.

3 The cars accelerate to reach their highest speed (maximum kinetic energy) at the bottom of the slope.

4 As the cars climb the slope on the other side, kinetic energy is converted back into GPE.

Throughout the ride, energy is being transformed into heat, light and sound.

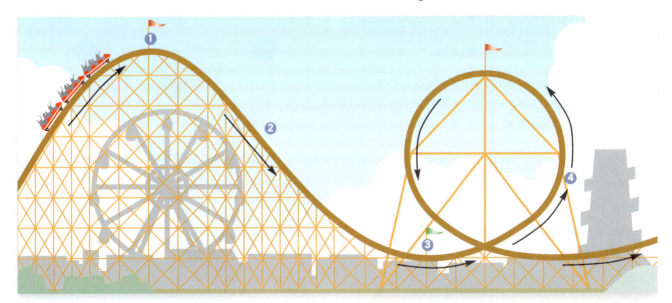

Key Words

Acceleration • Conservation of energy • Constant speed • Current • Electrical energy • Force • Gravitational potential energy • Kinetic energy • Mass • Potential energy • Speed • Velocity • Voltage

Roller Coasters and Relativity

Circular Motion

If you swing a rubber ball attached to a piece of string in a horizontal circle at **a constant speed**, the **direction** of the ball is always **changing**.

This means that the **velocity** of the ball is also **changing**, so the ball is undergoing constant **acceleration**.

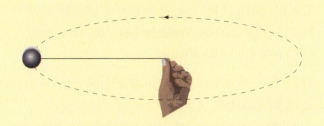

Centripetal Force

The acceleration is brought about by a resultant force acting on the object. The resultant force that acts on the ball to keep it moving in a circular path is an inward **centripetal force**, in this case, the tension in the string.

The same principle can be applied to…
* the Moon and satellites in orbit around the Earth
* the Earth moving in orbit around the Sun.

The Moon is kept in its orbit around the Earth, and in turn, the Earth is kept in its orbit around the Sun by an inward centripetal force: **gravity**.

Centripetal forces act in all cases of circular motion, for example, a car driving around a corner, the loop of a roller coaster ride, etc.

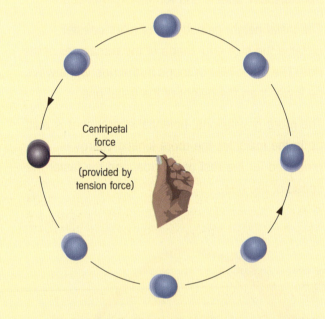

Centripetal force

(provided by tension force)

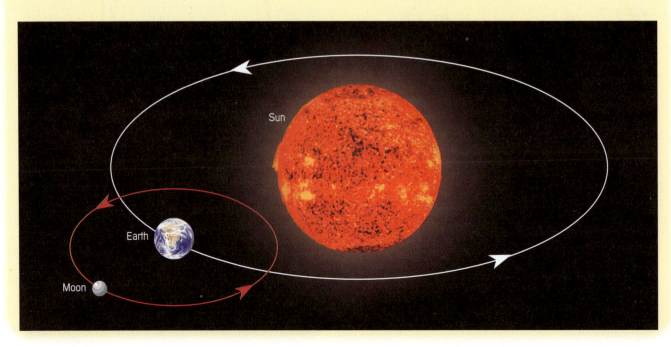

Sun

Earth

Moon

Work

When a force moves an object, **work is done** on the object, resulting in the **transfer of energy**:

Work done (J) = **Energy transferred (J)**

You can calculate the work done by using the following formula:

Work done (J) = **Force (N)** ✗ **Distance (m)**

Example

A man pushes a car with a steady force of 250N. The car moves a **distance** of 20m. How much work does the man do?

Work done = Force x Distance
= 250N x 20m = **5000J (5kJ)**

So, 5000J of **work has been done** and 5000J of **energy has been transferred**, since work done is equal to energy transferred.

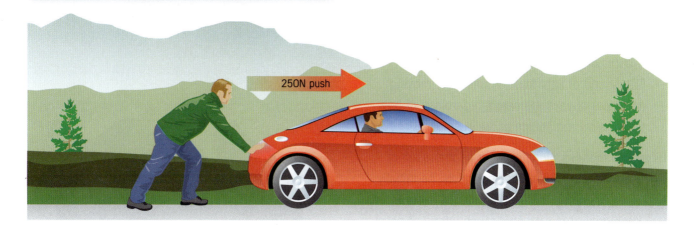

250N push

Power

Power is the **rate of doing work** or the **rate of transfer of energy**. The greater the power, the more work is done every second. Power is measured in **watts (W)** or **joules per second (J/s)**.

You can calculate power by using this formula:

Power = $\dfrac{\text{Work done (J)}}{\text{Time taken (s)}}$
$P = \dfrac{W}{t}$

For example, if two men of the same mass race up the same hill, they will do the same amount of work to reach the top.

But, since one man will have done the work in a shorter time, he will have a greater power.

Example

A crane lifts a load of 20 000N through a distance of 10m in 4s. Calculate the power of the crane.

> First, work out how much work the crane does against gravity, then find the power.

Work done = Force x Distance
= 20 000N x 10m = 200 000J

Power = $\dfrac{\text{Work done}}{\text{Time taken}}$

$= \dfrac{200\,000J}{4s}$ = **50 000W (or J/s) or 50kW**

Key Words

Distance • Energy transfer • Power • Resultant force • Work done

Roller Coasters and Relativity

Theories of Relativity

Theory of Relativity refers to the idea that time and space are relative concepts (i.e. they're dependent on something else).

In 1905, Einstein proposed the **Special Relativity Theory**, which led to the famous equation $E = mc^2$ (energy = mass x speed of light^2). This theory challenged the accepted ideas at that time and led to predictions that differed from those of Isaac Newton.

The theory is based on the following ideas:

- All movement is relative, for example, someone may be sitting still, but 'still' relative to what?
- Light has a constant speed (300 000km/s) in a particular direction.
- The speed of light from a constantly moving source is always the same, regardless of how fast or slow the source or the observer is moving.

Einstein's theories didn't emerge as the result of experimental data. Like other scientists, he initially explained his ideas using only **thought experiments** (i.e. imagination). It was only much later that proof was provided through careful experimental observations.

Some scientists are often reluctant to accept new theories, such as Einstein's theory of relativity, because they overturn long-established explanations.

Scientists may have carried out a lot of work and research based on other explanations, which they don't want to simply dismiss.

Theories such as Einstein's can also be difficult to prove, meaning that some scientists are more likely to continue basing their work on the long-established, accepted explanations.

Key Words
Theory of Relativity

HT Proving the Theories

Einstein's theory of relativity was accepted when results from **tests** were obtained that **proved** the theory.

For example, Einstein predicted that time is affected by gravity and that clocks in strong gravity tick slower than clocks in weaker gravity. So an experiment was carried out in which **atomic clocks** were placed at different distances from the surface of the Earth (i.e. at different gravitational strengths). Einstein's theory was proved to be correct.

Another of Einstein's predictions about the slowing down of time was experimentally proven by looking at high-energy **cosmic rays** that enter the Earth's atmosphere from space. As they're moving close to the speed of light, the count rate (average number of radioactive emissions) increased. This increase in count rate could only be explained by Einstein's theory.

Glossary of Key Words

Acceleration – the rate at which a body changes its velocity.

Conservation of energy – a law that states that energy can't be made or lost: it can only be changed from one form into another.

Constant speed – the speed of an object that is neither accelerating nor decelerating.

Current – the rate of flow of an electrical charge; measured in amperes (A).

Distance – the space between two points.

Electrical energy – energy of electric charges or current; measured in joules (J).

Energy transfer – a measure of how much work is done on an object.

Force – a push or pull acting on an object.

Gravitational potential energy (**GPE**) – one form of potential energy: the product of the weight of an object and its change in height; measured in joules (J).

Kinetic energy (**KE**) – the energy possessed by a moving object; measured in joules (J).

Mass – the quantity of matter in an object.

Potential energy (**PE**) – the energy stored in an object as a consequence of its position, shape or state (includes gravitational, electrical, nuclear and chemical); measured in joules (J).

Power – the rate of doing work or the rate of transfer of energy; measured in joules per second (J/s) or watts (W).

Speed – the rate at which a body moves.

Theory of Relativity – the theory that space and time are relative. The Special and General Theories were proposed by Albert Einstein and extended the work of Isaac Newton.

Velocity – the speed at which an object moves in a particular direction.

Voltage – the value of the potential difference between two points; measured in volts, V or millivolts, mV.

Work done – the product of the force applied to a body and the distance moved in the direction of the force; measured in joules (J).

HT **Resultant force** – the total force acting on an object (all the forces combined).

Practice Questions

1 PE = m x g x h

For each of the letters in the equation above…

i) write down what it stands for   **ii)** write down the units it's measured in.

a) PE **i)** ....   **ii)** ....

b) m   **i)** ....   **ii)** ....

c) g   **i)** ....   **ii)** ....

d) h   **i)** ....   **ii)** ....

2 A car of mass 1200kg is moving at a constant speed of 30m/s. How much kinetic energy does it have? Give your answer in kJ.

....

....

....

3 An electric kettle connected to the 240V mains supply draws a current of 10A. The kettle takes 2 minutes to boil some water. How much electrical energy is used? Give your answer in kJ.

....

....

....

4 What is the principle of the conservation of energy?

....

....

5 What happens after a roller coaster has reached its maximum height? Tick the **three** correct options.

A It loses kinetic energy as it descends

B It loses gravitational potential energy as it descends

C It gains momentum as it descends

D It reaches the same height on the next loop

E It loses energy due to friction, heat and sound

HT

6 Choose the correct words from the options given to complete the following sentences.

speed   acceleration   centrifugal   velocity   centripetal   direction

a) The inward force that keeps the Earth orbiting the Sun is called the _____ force.

b) The Earth moves at a constant _____ in its orbit, but its direction is always changing. This means its _____ is also changing, so the Earth is undergoing constant _____ .

7 What is the inward force that keeps the Moon in orbit around the Earth? _____

8 An arctic explorer pulls a sledge over some ice with a constant force of 250N, covering a distance of 5km. How much work has been done? Give your answer in kJ.

9 Which of the following statements are correct definitions of power? Tick the correct options.

A The rate of doing work ⬭   **B** The rate of change of momentum ⬭

C The rate of transfer of energy ⬭   **D** The amount of work done divided by time taken ⬭

10 A train takes 30 minutes to travel up an incline, gaining a height of 30m. It is pulling a load of 30 000N. Calculate the power of the train (ignore energy used to overcome friction).

11 Which of the following statements concern the theory of relativity? Tick the correct options.

A The speed of light is constant ⬭   **B** Light travels faster in a vacuum ⬭

C Nothing can go faster than the speed of light ⬭   **D** Time is affected by gravity ⬭

E All movement is relative ⬭

Putting Radiation to Use

The Atom

Atoms are the basic particles from which all matter is made. All chemical elements are made of atoms.

An atom has…

- a small **nucleus** consisting of **protons** (positively charged) and **neutrons** (neutral)
- electrons (negatively charged) that orbit the nucleus.

The **mass number** of an element is the total number of protons and neutrons in the nucleus of an atom.

The **atomic number** of an element is the number of protons in the nucleus (or electrons) in an atom.

The **atomic mass** is the mass of a particular atom compared to the mass of a carbon-12 atom.

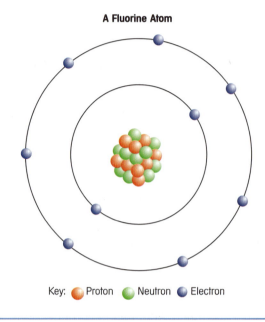

A Fluorine Atom

Key: ● Proton ● Neutron ● Electron

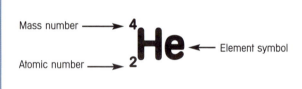

Mass number ⟶ 4

Atomic number ⟶ 2 **He** ⟵ Element symbol

HT Isotopes

The number of protons defines the element, so all atoms of a particular element have the same number of protons. This means that the **atomic (proton) number** is the same in all isotopes of an element.

Atoms of the same element can have a different number of neutrons. These atoms are called isotopes. This means that the **mass (nucleon) number** varies between isotopes. (Nucleon is the collective term for the number of protons and neutrons in the nucleus of an atom.)

For example, oxygen has three isotopes:

- oxygen-16 (^{16}O)
- oxygen-17 (^{17}O)
- oxygen-18 (^{18}O).

Mass number − Atomic number = Number of neutrons

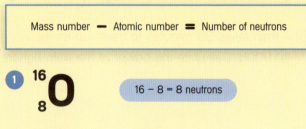

1 $^{16}_{8}O$ 16 − 8 = 8 neutrons

2 $^{17}_{8}O$ 17 − 8 = 9 neutrons

3 $^{18}_{8}O$ 18 − 8 = 10 neutrons

Radiation

When an **isotope** has an unstable nucleus (i.e. it has too many or too few neutrons), the nucleus will **split up** by randomly emitting **radiation**. Atoms of these isotopes are **radioactive**.

A radioactive nucleus will emit one of the following three types of radiation:

- **Alpha particle** (α) – a helium nucleus (a particle made up of two protons and two neutrons).
- **Beta particle** (β) – a high-energy electron.
- **Gamma ray** (γ) – high-frequency electromagnetic radiation.

The **activity** of a radioactive isotope is the average number of disintegrations that occur every second (becquerels). It decreases over a period of time.

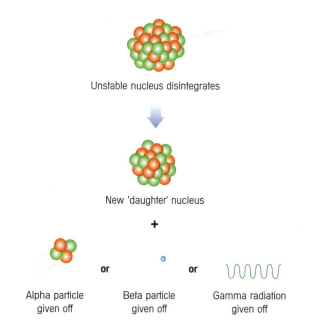

Unstable nucleus disintegrates

New 'daughter' nucleus

+

Alpha particle given off   **or**   Beta particle given off   **or**   Gamma radiation given off

Half-Life

The **half-life** of a radioactive isotope is a measurement of the rate of **radioactive decay**, i.e. the time it takes for half the nuclei to decay.

A radioactive isotope that has a very long half-life remains active for a very long time.

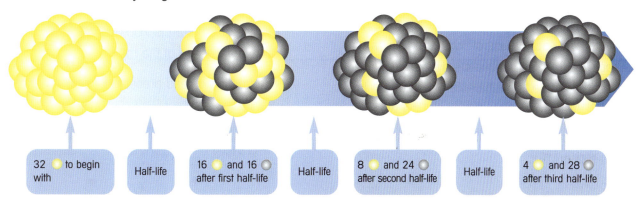

32 ⬤ to begin with

Half-life

16 ⬤ and 16 ⚪ after first half-life

Half-life

8 ⬤ and 24 ⚪ after second half-life

Half-life

4 ⬤ and 28 ⚪ after third half-life

⬤ = original atom
⚪ = new atom formed after original atom has decayed

N.B. This is a collection of atoms, not a nucleus.

Key Words

Alpha particle • Atom • Atomic mass • Atomic (proton) number • Beta particle • Gamma ray • Half-life • Isotopes • Mass (nucleon) number • Neutron • Nucleus • Proton • Radioactivity

Putting Radiation to Use

Using Half-Life

The graph below shows the count rate against time for the radioactive material iodine-128 (^{128}I):

- The **count rate** is the average number of radioactive emissions per second.
- As time goes on there are fewer and fewer unstable atoms left to decay.
- After 25 minutes the count rate has fallen to half its original value. Therefore, iodine-128 has a half-life of 25 minutes.

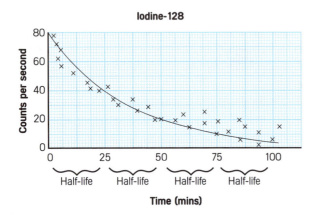

Knowledge about the **half-life** of a radioactive element can be used to date certain materials by measuring the amount of **radiation** they emit (radioactive dating).

Materials that contain radioactive isotopes decay to produce **stable isotopes**. If you know the **proportion** of each of these **isotopes** and the half-life of the **radioactive** isotope, then you can date the material:

- Igneous rocks may contain uranium isotopes that decay via a series of relatively short-lived isotopes to produce stable isotopes of lead. This takes a long time because uranium has a very long half-life.
- Wood and bones contain the carbon-14 ($^{14}_{7}$C) isotope, which decays when the organism dies.

It's important to remember that these methods require accurate experiments to measure the tiny quantities, which can lead to significant uncertainties in the date and age of materials.

Half-Life Calculations

Examples

1 A very small sample of dead wood has an activity of 1000 becquerels over a period of time. The same mass of 'live' wood has an activity of 4000 becquerels over an identical period of time. If the half-life of carbon-14 is 5730 years, calculate the age of the wood.

So, the carbon-14 has taken 2 x half-lives to decay to its present activity.

So, the age of the wood = 2 x 5730 years

= **11 460 years**.

2 A sample of igneous rock is found to contain three times as much lead as uranium. If the half-life of uranium is 700 000 000 years, calculate the age of the rock.

The fraction of lead present is $\frac{3}{4}$ while that of uranium is $\frac{1}{4}$.

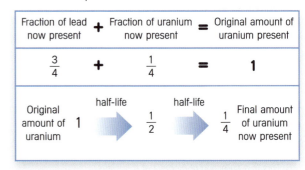

So, the age of the rock = 2 x half-life

= 2 x 700 000 000

= **1 400 000 000 years**

(1400 million years)

Putting Radiation to Use

Ionisation

When **radiation** collides with **neutral** atoms or molecules in a substance, the atoms or molecules may become charged due to **electrons** being 'knocked out' of their structure during the collision.

This alters their structure, leaving them as **ions** (atoms with an electrical charge) or **charged particles**.

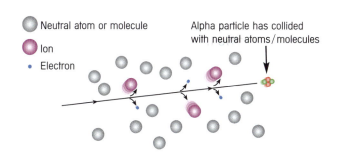

- ○ Neutral atom or molecule
- ● Ion
- • Electron

Alpha particle has collided with neutral atoms/molecules

Ionising and Penetrating Power

Each type of radiation has a different…

- **ionising power**
- ability to **penetrate** different materials
- range in air.

Only low activity sources are used in class demonstrations. They are kept in sealed lead-lined boxes and handled using tweezers or protective gloves.

HT Alpha particles, beta particles and gamma rays are **ionising radiations**. They're randomly emitted from the unstable nuclei of radioactive isotopes.

Particle	Description	Ionising Power	Penetrating Power
Alpha	2 protons, 2 neutrons, positive charge	Strong	Absorbed by a few centimetres of air, or thin paper.
Beta	Fast-moving electron, negative charge	Reasonable	Passes through air and paper. Absorbed by a few millimetres of aluminium.
Gamma	High-frequency electromagnetic waves, no charge	Weak	Very penetrating. Needs many centimetres of lead or metres of concrete to stop it.

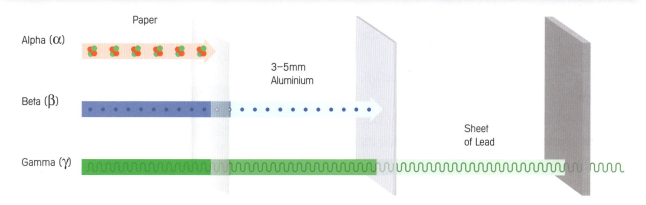

Paper

Alpha (α)

Beta (β)

3–5mm Aluminium

Gamma (γ)

Sheet of Lead

Key Words

Electron • Radioactive dating

Putting Radiation to Use

Uses of Radiation

Radiation can be used in the following situations:

- in smoke detectors
- to preserve food
- to sterilise medical instruments
- for diagnosis and treatment (in medicine).

Smoke Detectors

Most smoke alarms contain americium-241 which emits alpha radiation. The emitted alpha particles ionise the air particles. The ions formed are attracted to the oppositely charged electrodes, which causes a current to flow round the circuit.

When smoke enters the space between the two electrodes, fewer air particles are ionised because the alpha particles are absorbed by the smoke particles. This causes a smaller current than normal to flow, which triggers the alarm to sound.

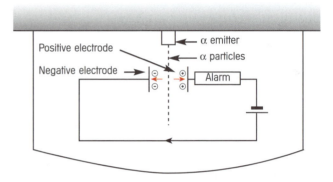

Preservation and Sterilisation

Food can be preserved by subjecting it to low doses of radiation. The radiation kills the microorganisms in the food, which prolongs its shelf life.

Gamma rays destroy microorganisms and bacteria, so they are used to sterilise medical instruments. An advantage of this method is that no heat is required, so damage to the instruments is minimised.

Diagnosis and Treatment

Ionising radiation can be used to treat tumours and cancers. The following methods are used:

- Radioactive material can be implanted in the area that needs to be treated.
- The patient can be dosed with a radioactive isotope.
- The patient can be exposed to precisely focused beams of radiation from a machine, such as an X-ray machine or gamma-ray emitter.

Radiotherapy is used to treat cancer because it slows down the spread or growth of cancerous cells.

Gamma rays and X-rays are forms of electromagnetic radiation. They can pass easily through flesh but not so easily through bone, which is why bones show up on an X-ray photograph.

	Ionising Power	Produced by...	Detected by...
Gamma rays	Weak	Unstable nuclei.	Scintillation counter
X-rays	Weak	Medical X-ray tubes (when fast-moving electrons hit a metal target).	Fast film (instant or within 10 minutes).

Putting Radiation to Use

Effects of Ionising Radiation

Ionising radiation can…
* **damage cells** and tissues, causing cancer, including leukaemia (cancer of the blood), or mutations (changes) in the cells
* result in the birth of **deformed babies** in future generations.

So, **precautions** must always be taken when dealing with any type of radiation.

With all types of radiation, the greater the dose received, the greater the risk of damage. But, the damaging effect depends on whether the radiation source is outside or inside the body.

Source Outside the Body

If the source of radiation is **outside** the body…
* alpha radiation is stopped by the skin and can't penetrate into the body
* beta and gamma radiation and X-rays can penetrate into the body to reach the cells of organs where they are absorbed.

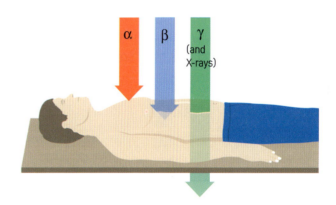

Source Inside the Body

If the source of radiation is **inside** the body…
* alpha radiation causes most damage because it's strongly absorbed by cells, causing the most ionisation
* beta and gamma radiation cause less damage as they are less likely to be absorbed by cells.

Key Words

Ionising radiation • Mutations • Sterilisation • X-rays

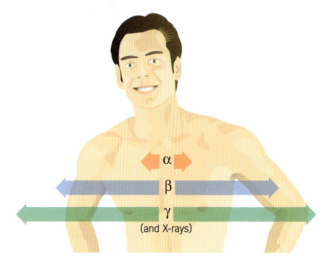

Putting Radiation to Use

HT Background Radiation

Background radiation is radiation that occurs naturally all around you. Improved understanding of the risks associated with radiation means that there is now little danger to your health. The pie chart shows the sources of background radiation.

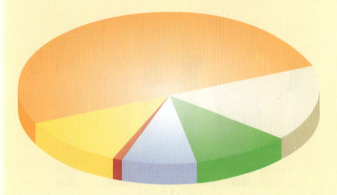

Radon gas (50%) is a colourless, odourless gas produced during the radioactive decay of uranium, which is found naturally in granite rock. Released at the surface of the ground, it poses a threat if it builds up in a home, e.g. it can result in lung cancer. The amount of radon varies. Areas built on granite, e.g. Devon, Cornwall, Aberdeen, tend to have a higher concentration.

Medical (12%), mainly X-rays.

Nuclear industry (less than 1%)

Cosmic rays (10%) from outer space and the Sun

Gamma rays (10%) from rock, soil and building products.

From food (12%)

Protecting the Earth

The Earth is surrounded by various layers of gas in the **atmosphere**. They shield and protect the Earth from radiation that comes from space, by **reflecting** the **radiation** back into space.

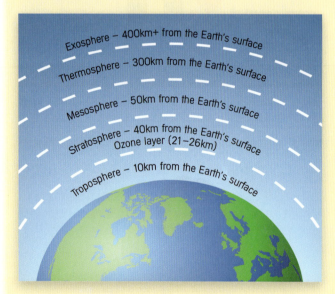

Exosphere – 400km+ from the Earth's surface

Thermosphere – 300km from the Earth's surface

Mesosphere – 50km from the Earth's surface

Stratosphere – 40km from the Earth's surface
Ozone layer (21–26km)

Troposphere – 10km from the Earth's surface

Increased knowledge about these layers has changed our scientific understanding of them in protecting Earth.

The Earth's **magnetic field** also protects us from the high-speed 'solar wind' that comes from the Sun. This magnetic field provides an invisible barrier to the charged particles that stream towards us and that are deflected by the field.

Without the atmospheric and magnetic fields, life on Earth wouldn't be possible.

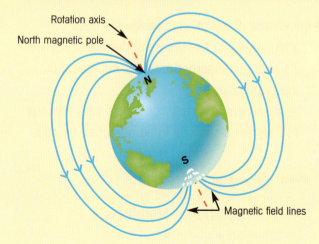

Rotation axis

North magnetic pole

N

S

Magnetic field lines

Key Words

Background radiation • Magnetic field • Radon gas

Glossary of Key Words

Alpha particle – consists of two protons and two neutrons (a helium nucleus); emitted from the nuclei of radioactive substances during alpha decay.

Atom – the smallest part of an element that displays the chemical property of the element; consists of a small central nucleus (containing protons and neutrons), surrounded by electrons.

Atomic mass – the mass of an atom compared to the mass of a carbon-12 atom.

Beta particle – fast-moving electron; emitted from the nuclei of radioactive substances during beta decay.

Electron – a negatively charged subatomic particle with a very tiny mass.

Gamma ray – electromagnetic radiation of a very high frequency emitted by excited nuclei.

Half-life – the time taken for half of the undecayed nuclei in radioactive material to decay.

Ionising radiation – a stream of high-energy particles / rays: alpha, beta, gamma; can damage human cells and tissues.

Isotopes – atoms of the same element that have the same number of protons but a different number of neutrons.

Mutation – a change in the structure of living cells.

Neutron – a neutrally charged subatomic particle with the same mass as a proton.

Nucleus – the centre of an atom containing protons and neutrons.

Proton – a positively charged subatomic particle with the same mass as a neutron.

Radioactive dating – a method of estimating the age of ancient objects, based on carbon-14 (for wood / bones) and uranium (for rocks).

Radioactivity – the emission of high-energy particles / rays from the spontaneous decay of unstable nuclei.

Sterilisation – destroying germs and bacteria by exposure to gamma rays.

X-rays – a form of electromagnetic radiation used in industry and medicine.

HT Atomic (proton) number – the number of protons in the nucleus of an atom.

Background radiation – radiation from natural sources in the environment.

Magnetic field – a field of force that exists around a magnetic body.

Mass (nucleon) number – the total number of protons and neutrons (nucleons) in the nucleus of an atom.

Radon gas – a colourless radioactive gas that occurs naturally.

Practice Questions

1. Which types of radiation does an unstable nucleus emit when it decays. Tick the **three** correct options.

   A   High-frequency electromagnetic radiation ⬭

   B   High-energy protons ⬭

   C   High-energy electrons ⬭

   D   Helium nuclei ⬭

2. Fill in the missing words to complete the following sentences.

   Alpha particles, ... and gamma rays are .... emitted from

   .... nuclei of radioactive isotopes.

3. What is meant by the term 'half-life'?

   ....

4. Two elements of uranium are $^{236}_{92}U$ and $^{235}_{92}U$.

   a) What do the numbers 235 and 236 represent?

   ....

   b) What does the number 92 represent?

   ....

   c) What are these elements of uranium called?

   ....

5. A sample of dead wood is found to have an activity of 3000 becquerels. A sample of live wood of equal mass has an activity of 4000 becquerels. The half-life of carbon-14 is 5730 years. How old is the wood?

   ....

   ....

6. Choose the correct words from the options given to complete the following sentence.

   protons   **electrons**   **neutral**   **positive**   **ions**   **nuclei**

   When radiation collides with .... atoms, it may alter their structure by knocking out

   .... and leaving them as charged particles or ....

7 Alpha, beta and gamma radiation can all ionise other atoms and penetrate materials but to different extents. Which row of the following table is correct?

	Most ionising	Most penetrating
A	Beta	Gamma
B	Beta	Beta
C	Alpha	Gamma
D	Gamma	Alpha
E	Alpha	Beta

8 Which of the following factors of ionising radiation pose an **increased** risk to health if it's increased? Tick the correct options.

- A The dose ◯
- B The activity ◯
- C The distance ◯
- D The half-life ◯

9 Which of the following applications does **not** use a radioactive isotope? Tick the correct option.

- A Smoke detection ◯
- B Sterilising ◯
- C Density control ◯
- D Food preservation ◯

HT

10 The following are various sources of background radiation. Number the sources **1–4** to place them in order, starting with the highest emitter.

- A Food ◯
- B Nuclear industry ◯
- C Cosmic rays ◯
- D Radon gas ◯

Power of the Atom

Predicting Energy Release

Large heavy **atoms**, for example, uranium, can become more **stable** by losing an **alpha** or **beta** particle. This process occurs naturally.

The tiny amount of mass lost in the **fission** process is translated into an enormous energy gain.

Einstein predicted the amount of energy that would be released by creating the following formula:

Energy	=	Mass	X	Speed of light²

$$E = mc^2$$

Einstein's predicted energy release was verified in 1943 when the first atomic bomb test was carried out.

Nuclear Fission

Stability can be gained more quickly by bombarding the nucleus of a uranium atom with neutrons to make it **split** in a process called **nuclear** fission.

These are the **products** of the collision:

- two smaller, 'daughter' nuclei
- two or more **neutrons**
- release of an enormous amount of **energy**.

Each fission reaction produces an enormous amount of energy. The neutrons produced can go on to interact with further ^{235}U nuclei, producing even more neutrons each time in a process called chain reaction.

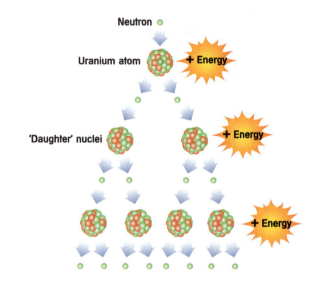

Neutron

Uranium atom   + Energy

'Daughter' nuclei   + Energy

+ Energy

Chain Reactions

Chain reactions can be manipulated and used in different ways. In an uncontrolled chain reaction, for example, an **atomic bomb**…

- neutrons bombard pure uranium nuclei
- an enormous amount of energy is released
- an enormous amount of radiation is released.

In a controlled chain reaction, for example, in a nuclear reactor…

- neutrons bombard a mixture of uranium-235 (^{235}U), uranium-238 (^{238}U) and plutonium-239 (^{239}Pu) nuclei
- the heat produced is used to generate electricity.

HT Decay Series

^{235}U decays naturally by alpha (➡) and beta (➡) emission to produce lead that's stable. This is the decay series:

^{235}U ➡ ^{231}Th ➡ ^{231}Pa ➡ ^{227}Ac ➡ ^{223}Fr ➡ ^{223}Ra ➡ ^{219}Rn ➡ ^{215}Po ➡ ^{211}Pb ➡ ^{211}Bi ➡ ^{207}Tl ➡ ^{207}Pb (Stable)

Power of the Atom

Nuclear Reactors and Waste

These are the key features of a **pressurised water reactor** (**PWR**):

- The reactor is inside a steel pressure vessel, surrounded by thick concrete to **absorb radiation**.
- Heat (thermal energy) from the reactor is carried away by water that's boiled to produce steam.
- The steam drives the turbines that generate **electricity** (electrical energy).
- The steam cools to produce water, which is then returned to the reactor to be **re-heated**.
- The chain reactions are **controlled** by lowering metal rods in between the uranium fuel rods. The rods absorb neutrons and so reduce or stop the reaction.

The products of nuclear fission are radioactive, and remain radioactive for a long time, which means they must be reprocessed or stored very carefully:

- **Low-level waste** is sealed and buried in landfill sites.
- **Higher-level waste** is mixed with sugar, bonded with glass, poured into steel cylinders and kept underground.

Key Words

Chain reaction • Daughter nucleus • Decay series • Electrical energy • Fission • Neutron • Nuclear reactor • Nucleus • Radioactive • Thermal energy

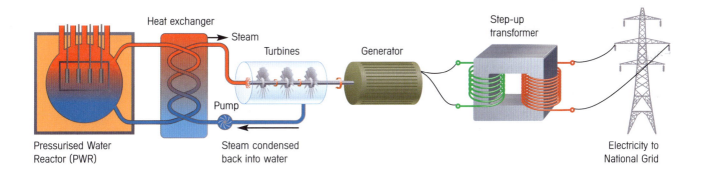

Heat exchanger — Steam — Turbines — Generator — Step-up transformer — Electricity to National Grid — Pump — Steam condensed back into water — Pressurised Water Reactor (PWR)

Environmental and Social Impacts

The use of **nuclear power** has advantages and disadvantages. Setting up a nuclear power station in any part of the UK will have a huge environmental and social impact.

Here are some of the **advantages** of nuclear power:

- No greenhouse gas emissions, e.g. CO_2.
- No air pollutants, e.g. CO, SO_2.
- Small quantity of waste.
- Low fuel costs.
- Local economy could benefit from the many jobs created.

Here are some of the **disadvantages** of nuclear power:

- Risk of a major accident, e.g. Six Mile Island, Chernobyl.
- Nuclear waste is dangerous and long-lived, which leads to transport and storage problems.
- High construction and maintenance costs.
- Security concerns, e.g. risk of terrorist attack.
- Large areas of land used.
- Spoils the look of the countryside.
- Destroys wildlife habitats.
- Would mean an increase in traffic, noise and air pollution.

Power of the Atom

HT Nuclear Fusion

Nuclear fusion involves the joining together of two or more atomic nuclei to form a larger atomic nucleus.

It takes a huge amount of heat and energy to force the nuclei to fuse. This means that fusion isn't a practical way to generate power.

But, the energy produced by fusion is much greater than that produced by fission and, if we could somehow harness the energy from fusion, we would have unlimited amounts of energy and our energy problems would be solved.

The energy produced by the Sun, and similar stars, comes from the fusion of two 'heavy' isotopes of hydrogen called **deuterium** and **tritium**.

To push and join the two nuclei together is difficult and requires very high temperatures, high pressures and high densities, similar to those found in the Sun and similar stars.

In the core of the Sun, hydrogen is converted to helium by fusion. This provides the energy to keep the Sun burning.

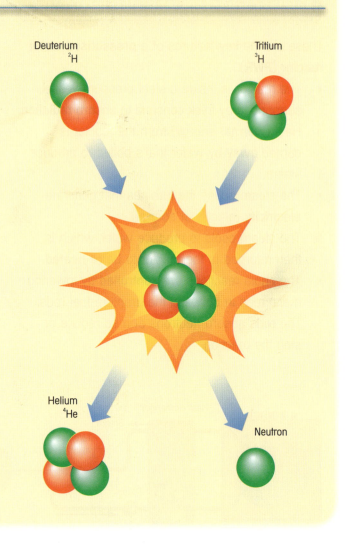

Cold Fusion

A large amount of work is currently being done on understanding the processes involved in **cold fusion**.

Cold fusion is said to occur at much lower temperatures than ordinary fusion. In order to overcome the repulsive forces between nuclei, cold fusion involves different nuclei from those that take place in ordinary nuclear fusion.

Current scientific theories on cold fusion will not be fully accepted until they have been **validated** (proven) by experimental evidence provided by the scientific community.

Key Words
Attraction • Electrostatic • Fusion • Insulation • Repulsion

Electrostatic Charge

Materials (e.g. metals) that allow electricity to flow through them easily are called **conductors**.

Materials, for example, plastics, that don't allow electricity to flow through them are called insulators.

Electrostatic (static) is electricity that stays on a material and doesn't move. Insulating material can become charged with static if there's **friction** between it and another insulator. This causes **electrons** (which have a negative charge) to be rubbed off one insulator onto the other:

- The material **receiving** electrons becomes **negatively** charged.
- The material **giving up** electrons becomes **positively** charged.

If you rub a Perspex rod with a cloth, it loses electrons to become positively charged. The cloth gains electrons to become negatively charged.

If you rub an ebonite rod with a fur, it gains electrons to become negatively charged. The fur loses electrons to become positively charged.

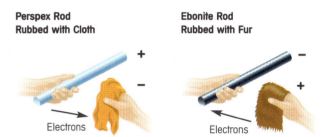

Perspex Rod Rubbed with Cloth

Ebonite Rod Rubbed with Fur

Electrons   Electrons

Repulsion and Attraction

When two charged materials are brought together, they exert a **force** on each other. They can either be attracted or repelled:

1. Two materials with the **same** type of **charge**, for example, two Perspex rods, will **repel** each other.
2. Two materials with **different** types of **charge**, for example, an ebonite rod and a Perspex rod, will be **attracted** to each other.

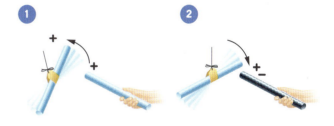

Common Electrostatic Phenomena

The following are common examples of electrostatic in everyday life:

- **Cars** can become charged due to friction between it and the air when it moves. This is why you can sometimes get a shock from a car after a journey.
- **Synthetic fabrics** can charge each other. You can see sparks of static discharging when you separate the materials.
- **Clouds** become charged by rising hot air. They discharge by producing a bolt of lightning.

Power of the Atom

Uses of Electrostatic Charge

Electrostatic charge can be used to create **fingerprint** images. Fingerprints are patterns of ridges and valleys in the skin:

- Ridges give high electrostatic charges.
- Valleys give small electrostatic charges.

The semiconductor fingerprint sensor measures the electrostatic charge between the sensor surface and the skin. The charges are then copied onto a sensor to create an image.

Electrostatic charge is also used in **laser printers**:

1. A tiny laser spot is scanned across the surface of a revolving drum (the photoreceptor), which is positively charged.
2. The laser light discharges certain points on the surface of the drum to reveal an electrostatic image to be printed.
3. The drum is then coated with black toner (which is positively charged).
4. The drum rolls over the (negatively charged) paper, which picks up the exact image.
5. The image is fixed to the paper.

Dangers of Electrostatic Charge

Electrostatic charge can be **dangerous** in certain situations, for example, when **refuelling aircraft**.

As the fuel passes along the pipe it gains electrons from the pipe. This results in the pipe becoming positively charged and the fuel becoming negatively charged.

The resulting **voltage** (potential difference) between the two can cause a **spark** (discharge), which could cause a huge **explosion**.

To prevent an explosion, either of the following can be done:

- The fuel tank can be earthed with a copper conductor.
- The tanker and the plane can be linked with a copper conductor.

Glossary of Key Words

Attraction – the drawing together of two materials with different charges.

Chain reaction – a self-sustaining series of reactions, like nuclear fission, in which the neutrons released in one fission trigger the fission of other nuclei.

Daughter nucleus – a nucleus that is produced by the radioactive decay of another nucleus (i.e. a larger, parent nucleus).

Electrical energy – a form of energy given by the product of the electric charge and the potential difference (voltage).

Electrostatic – the stationary electric field that surrounds a charged object; caused by friction.

Fission – the splitting of atomic nuclei that produces a large amount of energy.

Fusion – the joining together of atomic nuclei that produces a large amount of energy.

Insulation – when electricity (or heat) can't flow easily.

Nucleus – the core of an atom; contains protons and neutrons.

Neutron – a neutrally charged subatomic particle found in the nucleus of an atom.

Nuclear reactor – a device in which a nuclear fission chain reaction is controlled to produce energy in the form of electricity.

Radioactive – materials containing unstable nuclei that spontaneously decay.

Repulsion – the equal pushing away of two materials with the same type of charge.

Thermal energy – heat energy.

HT **Decay series** – shows how particular radioactive nuclei decay to produce stable nuclei.

Practice Questions

1 The energy (E) released in nuclear fission can be found using Einstein's equation.

    a) Write down the equation. ....

    b) Other than E, explain the symbols used.

        i) ....   **ii)** ....

2 Write down whether each of the following statements describes nuclear **fission** or nuclear **fusion**.

    a) Joins two or more nuclei together ....

    b) Produces 'daughter' nuclei ....

    c) Produces two or more neutrons ....

    d) Uses tritium ....

3 What is meant by the term 'chain reaction'?

....

....

4 **a)** Give two advantages to the environment of a nuclear power station.

        i) ....

        ii) ....

    b) Give two disadvantages to the environment of a nuclear power station.

        i) ....

        ii) ....

5 What are the two levels of waste produced by nuclear fission reactors?

    a) ....

    b) ....

HT

6 Nuclear fusion involves the joining together of deuterium (^{2}H) and tritium (^{3}H). What three products are produced in the fusion Reaction?

    a) ....   **b)** ....   **c)** ....

HT

7 Which of the following conditions are necessary for a fusion reaction? Tick the **three** correct options.

    A Low temperature ☐

    B High densities ☐

    C High pressure ☐

    D High mass nuclei ☐

    E High temperature ☐

8 Fill in the missing words to complete the following sentences.

    a) If an ebonite rod is moved near a suspended Perspex rod, the suspended rod will be

    _____ .

    b) If you move a Perspex rod near a suspended Perspex rod, the suspended rod will be

    _____ .

9 Choose the correct words from the options given to complete the following sentences.

fur   Perspex   electrons   electrostatic   negatively   cloth   protons   positively   ebonite

    a) An _____ charge is an area of charge that clings to a material and

    doesn't move.

    b) A material receiving _____ becomes _____ charged.

    c) An example of this is when an _____ rod is rubbed with _____ .

10 The following statements show how a laser printer works. Number the statements **1–5** to put them in the correct order.

    A Paper is given a positive charge ☐

    B Drum is given a positive charge ☐

    C Laser beam shines on drum discharging certain points ☐

    D Printer coats drum with black toner ☐

    E Drum rolls over paper to pick-up image ☐

11 Why do appliances need to be earthed?

_____

Answers to Practice Questions

Inside Living Cells

1. B and C
2. A5; B2; C1; D4; E3
3.
   mRNA — Chemical found in the nucleus of a cell
   RNA — Carries specific amino acids to the ribosome
   rRNA — Takes a copy of the genetic code to the cytoplasm
   tRNA — Found in ribosomes
   DNA — A single stranded molecule involved in protein synthesis
4. Insulin gene identified, removed using restriction enzyme. Human DNA inserted in plasmid. Bacteria divide. Cultivated in fermenter.
5. **a)–e) In any order:** Aseptic conditions; Nutrients; Temperature; pH; Oxygen; Agitation
6. D
7. oxygen / glucose; glucose / oxygen; cells; Enzymes; energy
8. Aerobic respiration uses oxygen to release energy from glucose / food. Anaerobic respiration doesn't use oxygen to release energy from glucose / food.
9. When someone is very overweight.
10. All the basic food groups in the correct proportions for an individual's needs.

Divide & Develop

1. a) Most parts of the body
   b) Four cells
   c) Genetically different
   d) Two sets per nucleus
   e) Cell replacement and growth
2. A2; B4; C1; D3.
3.
   Chromosome — A section of DNA that controls a feature
   Diploid — A long strand of DNA
   Gene — A type of cell division
   Haploid — A cell nucleus with two sets of chromosomes
   Mitosis — A cell nucleus with one set of chromosomes
4. Cell division is when cells divide to make more cells. Cell expansion is when cells get bigger.
5. **a)–c) In any order:** Genes / inheritance; Hormones; Nutrition / diet.
6. They increase body mass and strength.
7. a) They are not specialised.
   b) There is no limit to the number of times they can divide, they can carry on dividing.
8. D
9. A2; B5; C1; D4; E3
10. C
11. **a)–b) Any two from:** To improve immune response to diseases; To make cancer cells more sensitive to treatment; To make healthy cells more resistant to anti-cancer drugs; To inject cancer cells with genes that can destroy them.

Energy Flow

1. A, C and D
2. A3; B1; C2
3. C
4. B
5. C
6. releases; carbon dioxide; removes
7. a) soil; nitrates
   b) Decomposers
   c) nitrogen; ammonium
8. Fertilizers on fields are washed into streams / rivers / ponds. This causes extreme growth of aquatic plants, so light is blocked off. Plants die, decomposers use up oxygen and everything dies.
9. Carbon dioxide / methane released into the air insulate the Earth. More and more heat is trapped and the global temperature rises.
10. Food is provided, predators are excluded, fish are in a confined space and diseases are chemically controlled.
11. Provide a controlled environment: optimum light, optimum temperature, optimum carbon dioxide, pests are controlled, water is provided.

Answers to Practice Questions

Interdependence

1. **a) i)–iii) Any three from:** Insulation for heat retention; Small surface area to volume ratio for heat retention; Whitish coat for camouflage to hide from prey; Strong legs for swimming; Large feet to spread weight on ice.
    b) i)–iii) Any three from: Large surface area to volume ratio for heat loss; Little body fat so no insulation for heat retention; Lose little water through urine and sweat – retain the little water there is; Can drink lots in one go.

2. Interdependence — The relationship between organisms where one organism depends on another for a resource
    Competition — Rivalry between organisms for a resource that they both need
    Resource — Something that is used by an organism
    Predation — The process of predators hunting their prey
    Population — A group of organisms of the same species
    Adaptation — Something that makes an organism better able to survive

3. Air is less dense at altitude. There's less oxygen. Extra red blood cells mean oxygen is transported more efficiently.

4. Contamination of the environment by waste products of human activity.

5. D

6. A, B and E

7. A species may be unable to adapt to the change / unable to evolve. The species becomes endangered due to death, which can lead to extinction.

8. They are sensitive to sulphur dioxide – high levels kill them.

9. **a)–c) In any order:** Floods; Changes in weather patterns; Droughts

10. Ozone filters out UV light. CFCs damage the ozone layer. UV light can cause skin cancer.

Synthesis

1. **a)** Aqueous **b)** Solid **c)** Gas **d)** Liquid
2. A compound that only contains hydrogen and carbon.
3. An alkane is a saturated hydrocarbon and an alkene is an unsaturated hydrocarbon containing a double covalent carbon–carbon bond.
4. The alkene will decolourise the bromine water.
5. **a)–c) Any three suitable answers, e.g.:** In the manufacture of methylated spirits; In greener fuels, e.g. Gasohol; As a solvent in cosmetics and perfumes.
6. Thermal decomposition
7. Thermoplastics can be softened and remoulded into new shapes. Thermosetting polymers have strong bonds between the chains so can't be re-softened or reshaped.
8. **a)–c) In any order:** Adding plasticisers; Adding stabilisers; Adding cross-linking agents.
9. Cooking; unsaturated; liquids; temperature; high; fats.
10. To raise its melting point and increase its shelf life.
11. A
12. They are important for sustainable development as they prevent waste.
13. Three (nitrogen monoxide, nitrogen dioxide and nitric acid are useful; water is not useful).
14. C
15. **a)** Calculated from the masses of atoms.
    b) Actual mass obtained from the reaction in the experiment.

In Your Element

1. C
2. B
3. From the average of the different isotopes of an element.
4. electrons; nucleus.
5. **a)** 1 **b)** 3 **c)** 5
6. **a)** electrons; outer. **b)** Electrons; atoms.
7. LiO_2
8. Cations are positively charged (and attracted to the negative electrode). Anions are negatively charged (and attracted to the positive electrode).
9. A salt that is made from anions and cations.
10. $2O^{2-}(g) \rightarrow O_2(g) + 4e^-$
11. B, D and E.

Answers to Practice Questions

Chemical Structures

1. **a)** non-metal; strong; shared.
    b) atoms; molecules.
2. 3 pairs
3. 2 atoms join together.
4. **a)−b) In any order:** Strong covalent bonds in the molecule; Weak forces between the molecules.
5. **Accept any suitable answer, e.g.:** Inter-molecular forces between the atoms are very strong; The molecules do not come apart very easily; When it boils the covalent bonds within the molecules don't break.
6. Diamond
7. C, D, and F.
8. Their electrons can move freely within the structure and carry the electric charge.

9. A, B and D.
10. C
11. **a)−b) In any order:** It's hard to see how atoms are arranged in the structure; It's hard to see how electrons are arranged in the atom.
12. destroy; infections; tuberculosis.
13. **a)−c) In any order:** Replace substances deficient or missing from the body; Alter activity of cells; Destroy infectious microorganisms or abnormal cells.
14. People believe they experience relief following the administration of an unreactive substance.

How Fast? How Furious?

1. **a)−c) Any three from:** Increase temperature; Increase surface area; Increase concentration; Use a catalyst.
2. A and C.
3. When reacting particles collide with each other with sufficient energy to react.
4. The frequency and energy of collisions increases.
5. **Any one from:** activation; minimum.
6. A biological catalyst.
7. Exothermic - More energy is released when new bonds are formed than is needed to break bonds.
    Endothermic - Requires more energy to break bonds than is released when new bonds are formed.
8. **a)** reversible; products.
    b) increase; decrease.

9. It will never reach completion.
10. **a)−c) In any order:** Temperature of 450°C; Pressure of 200 atmospheres; Iron catalyst.
11. It reaches a state of dynamic equilibrium.
12. **a)** **i)−ii) Accept any two suitable answers, e.g.:** They are produced to match crop requirements; They are easier to store, distribute and handle than organic alternatives.
    b) **i)−ii) Accept any two suitable answers, e.g.:** They use and recycle natural waste; They encourage good soil structure and management.
13. **a)** It becomes a positively charged ion.
    b) It becomes a negatively charged ion.

As Fast As You Can!

1. **a)** velocity; speed; direction
    b) magnitude; vector
2. **a)** 200m/s (Velocity = $\dfrac{\text{Distance}}{\text{Time}}$ = $\dfrac{36\,000\text{m}}{3 \times 60\text{s}}$
    = 200m/s vertically)
    b) 0m (since it returns to the same point)
3. **a)** rate; velocity
    b) vector; m/s^2
4. **a)** 2m/s^2 (Acceleration = $\dfrac{\text{Change in velocity}}{\text{Time}}$ = $\dfrac{10-0}{5}$
    = 2m/s^2)
    b) The line has a constant slope or gradient.
5. **a)**

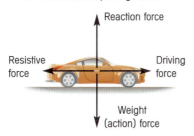

6. 1 200 000 kg m/s (Momentum = Mass x Velocity = 100 000kg x 12m/s = 1 200 000 kg m/s)

b) The car will decelerate (slow down).
7. A, C and D
8. A, B, C and D
9. **a)** **i)** Upward force of air resistance
    ii) Downward force of weight
    b) Resultant force is zero, no acceleration, falling speed is constant, reaches terminal velocity.

Roller Coasters and Relativity

1. **a)** **i)** Potential energy
    ii) J (joule)
   b) **i)** Mass
    ii) kg
   c) **i)** Gravitational field strength
    ii) N/kg or m/s^2
   d) **i)** Change in height
    ii) m
2. 540kJ (Kinetic energy = $\frac{1}{2}$ x Mass x Velocity^2 = $\frac{1}{2}$ x 1200kg
   x $(30m/s)^2$ = 600 x 900 = 540 000 = 540kJ)
3. 288kJ (Electrical energy = Voltage x Current x Time = 240V x 10A
   x (2 x 60)s = 288 000J = 288kJ)
4. Energy can't be made or lost, only changed from one form into another.
5. B, C and E

6. **a)** centripetal
   b) speed; velocity; acceleration
7. Gravity
8. 1250kJ (Work done = Force x Distance moved = 250N x 5000m
   = 1 250 000J = 1250kJ)
9. A, C and D
10. Work done = Force x Distance moved = 30 000N x 30m
    = 900 000J

    Power = $\frac{\text{Work done}}{\text{Time taken}}$ = $\frac{900\,000J}{(30 \times 60)s}$ = 500W

11. A, C, D and E

Putting Radiation to Use

1. A, C and D
2. Beta particles; randomly; unstable.
3. The time it takes for half the nuclei of a radioactive isotope to decay.
4. **a)** The mass (nucleon) number; i.e. total number of protons and neutrons.
   b) The atomic (proton) number; i.e. number of protons or electrons.
   c) Isotopes of uranium.
5. 2865 years (4000 → 2000 is 1 half-life; 4000 → 3000 is $\frac{1}{2}$
   half-life = $\frac{1}{2}$ x 5730 = 2865 years.)

6. neutral; electrons; ions
7. C
8. A, B and D
9. C
10. A 2; B 4; C 3; D 1

Power of the Atom

1. **a)** E = mc^2
   b) **i)-ii) In any order:** m = mass; c = speed of light.
2. **a)** Fusion
   b) Fission
   c) Fission
   d) Fusion
3. When neutrons bombard a uranium nucleus that splits, forming two smaller nuclei and two or more neutrons that go on to split other uranium nuclei.
4. **a)** **i)-ii) In any order:** No greenhouse gas emissions; small quantity of waste **or any other suitable answer**
   b) **i)-ii) In any order:** Destroys large areas of land and wildlife; waste is dangerous and long-lived **or any other suitable answer**
5. **a)-b) In any order:** low-level waste; high-level waste

6. **a)-c) In any order:** Helium (4He); Neutrons; Energy
7. B, C and E
8. **a)** attracted
   b) repelled
9. **a)** electrostatic
   b) electrons; negatively
   c) ebonite; fur
10. A 4; B 1; C 2; D 3; E 5
11. To allow electrons to flow from one body to another to remove an imbalance of charge or build up of charge.

Notes